EXPLOITS
IN THE
MIRACULOUS

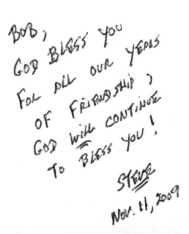

BOB,
GOD BLESS YOU
FOR ALL OUR YEARS
OF FRIENDSHIP)
GOD WILL CONTINUE
TO BLESS YOU !

STEVE
Nov. 11, 2009

EXPLOITS
IN THE
MIRACULOUS

STEVE BUZA

Outskirts Press, Inc.
Denver, Colorado

Exploits in the Miraculous
All Rights Reserved.
Copyright © 2009 Steve Buza
V3.0 R2.0

Outskirts Press, Inc.
http://www.outskirtspress.com

ISBN: 978-1-4327-4342-0

Outskirts Press and the "OP" logo are trademarks belonging to Outskirts Press, Inc.

PRINTED IN THE UNITED STATES OF AMERICA

Dedication

To my precious wife Sharon.
To my children: Sherry, Steve III,
Sarah, and Sabrina.
To my thirteen grandchildren.

Table of Contents

Foreword

If I were diagnosed with a terminal illness, there is only one man in the world I would call to minister the gift of healing on my behalf, and that man is Steve Buza, the author of the book you are about to read. I say that because I have had the privilege to minister with Steve and witness first-hand the healing anointing that God uses in such extraordinary ways through him.

I have been by Steve's side as he spoke a new brain into a brain-dead man whose wife the physicians were pressuring to pull the plug. Every word of faith that Steve spoke to the comatose man was fulfilled and, in less than a week, that man walked out of the hospital and lived many years in good health.

While in Jamaica, walking on the dirt paths worn between lean-to sheet metal shacks, I witnessed Steve speak healing to a deaf girl, who then was able to hear for the first time. I will never forget seeing the joy on her face, and then on her parents' faces, after she ran to tell them the good news. Suddenly it seemed, the whole village lined up in front of Steve for healing.

Once in our church, after a service was over, Steve came to me and said that God was going to lengthen three legs. I took the microphone and spoke that word to the remaining handful of people. I must admit my faith was not very high for anything supernatural to happen. Soon two people came forward and we watched their legs lengthen as Steve ministered healing. Later some parents brought in their son who had been playing in the church playground. This boy was born with a shorter leg and walked with a slight limp. He was also ridiculed at school because of the funny way he ran. Steve sat him down in a chair, took hold of his foot and commanded the leg to grow in the name of Jesus. Immediately the boy's calf muscle began to twitch and his leg began to shake as we watched that leg grow out as quickly as Pinocchio's nose! As soon as it was completed, he jumped up and ran around the sanctuary as any normal child would!

Such are just a few of the miraculous healings I witnessed by the side of Steve Buza. The stories you will read are true. God has not changed: He is a healing God and Steve Buza is a man of extraordinary faith who God continues to use. This book is not about a world renowned evangelist or of a powerful minister of the past. Steve is a business owner who ministers healing in the course of his daily life. Often he prays for his customers who are immediately and divinely healed! However, you do not need Steve Buza to pray for your miracle: You can learn to do it for yourself, as I have. You too can believe and minister God's wonderful gift of healing. It is a sign that should follow every believer. Let this book be your textbook to learn how to claim your healing and minister in this wonderful powerful God-given gift.

Dr. J. Lee Simmons, founding Pastor of Faith Chapel of Syracuse, New York and President of Living Faith Global Ministries

Introduction

When the Lord started using me many years ago in the miraculous, my wife and I could hardly take it all in. We soon realized that seeing salvations, healings and signs and wonders were only part of a "normal" Christian life in the Kingdom of God.

I always got excited when I would read about the exploits of Smith Wigglesworth, John G. Lake, T.L. Osborn, Oral Roberts and many others. With all my heart I wanted to be like them and touch people's lives.

As you read the stories in this book, I pray that you will realize that God is willing and ready to move you into new dimensions of the supernatural--beyond anything you can possibly imagine.

Let's get ready to be used greatly of the Lord!

If you are helping people in a Christian service, or in a secular setting, I believe--if you have the Holy Spirit with you as you minister and you let **Him** move as **He desires**-- you will have the "Bible Days" power flowing like a river.

Note:

Where appropriate some names were changed in this book in order to protect privacy.

1

The Early Years

I was born in Syracuse, New York during WWII. At the time my father was in the US Army and was stationed in Europe for most of my first years of life.

I was raised in the Assembly of God church, along with my younger brother, Rich, and sisters, Robin and Linda. My father served as the church Music Director and was a talented musician playing both piano and organ.

When I was fourteen my parents divorced and my father remarried. The divorce was very traumatic for me and it was many years before I could forgive my father for leaving. If you divorce, it hurts many lives because you really break-up your whole family.

Over thirty years later dad called my mother

from the hospital before he died. He told her that he realized that he had played the part of a fool. He said he couldn't leave this earth without asking her forgiveness. He told her that if he had to do it all over again he would never have left her. She had never fallen out of love with him and remained single all of her life.

Another event that impacted my childhood, in a positive way, took place before my parents' divorce. Dad took a week off work and took the family down to Harrisburg, PA. We attended the tent meetings of the great evangelist Oral Roberts. Two years later Rev. Roberts came to the fairgrounds in Syracuse for another week. We also went to those meetings.

Perhaps I should have known then that the Lord was going to use me in miraculous ways because I loved what I saw. From a young age I was always interested in the supernatural. I was in awe when I saw Oral Roberts pray for a little deaf girl. He then walked further and further away from the child saying in a whisper, "Can you hear me now? Can you hear me now?" It excited me tremendously when she replied, "Yes! Yes!" I thought: *Wow, I'd like to help a little child like that some day!* The miraculous was what impacted me about Oral

Roberts' ministry. I wasn't drawn to his preaching. I couldn't wait for him to get through his sermon and get to the healing part. That was because I had been brought up in a church that talked about the healing power of God but I never saw any of it. I grew up hearing the refrain from an old hymn, "There's power, power, wonder-working power in the blood…" sung in our church, but I can't say I really saw a lot of that power ever manifested.

Now I saw Oral Roberts walk into his tent, pull up a folding chair and say, "I'm here tonight to heal you people if you will agree in faith with me and the Holy Spirit." I thought, "Wow, here is a man that believes this stuff can really happen!"

I continued to go to church regularly throughout my teen years, mainly because my grandmother required it and she took me with her. My grandmother and mother were very active in the church. As my mother did not drive, my grandmother drove us every week.

After I finished high school at age 18, I started working for Colonial Construction Company. Harry Goldberg was the owner and for 21 years my dad was his executive vice president. Dad was in charge of over 120 men.

I was relatively new to doing construction work

but I picked it up very quickly. So quickly that after only two months I ran my own crew. The company had 68 salesmen. We did home remodeling throughout the state of New York. If they sold a job in the Catskills I would go there and live out of a suitcase for a month. Then, if they sold something up in the Adirondacks, I would go there. We had jobs all over the state.

Mr. Goldberg was a very wonderful employer and I had favor with him because of my dad. He thought the world of my dad and that's why he made him his right-hand man. That didn't hurt me in any respect. Mr. Goldberg also saw I had a good work ethic. I got that from my dad and my grandfather who were both hard workers.

When I was young and single, I went to church and had a Christian upbringing but I wasn't serving the Lord. I was away from home for long periods of time working construction. Looking back on it, though, I can see the Lord's protective hand on me. Alcohol never touched my lips. When working with construction crews there's usually drinking, smoking, cussing and womanizing. I had no control over whether or not my crew went to a local bar after work. But, even though I wasn't serving the Lord, God kept me from doing those things. I just wanted to rest and get ready for the next day. I would go to the room and watch TV. I wasn't tempted to womanize. There were some opportunities to go in that direction had I wanted to: I just had no desire to cross that boundary.

How I Met My Wife

I was almost 20 years old at the time I first met Sharon. My father and Lydia felt a certain amount of guilt about how they started their relationship. They were pretty well known in Christian circles in Syracuse, so they felt it was best to get a fresh start and started going to church in Auburn about 23 miles to the west of Syracuse. They started attending the Second Baptist Church there. My siblings and I would attend with them when we stayed every other weekend at their home. I wasn't really serving the Lord. I was just going through the motions. I had attended about six weeks when a young lady there named Sharon Adams came up with an idea. She saw me sitting on the end of the row. I never had a Bible with me so she came up with an ingenious plan in order to meet me. She asked the usher, "Would you give my Bible to that young man on the end of the row?" assuming I would return it to her after the service. She assumed right because she became my wife. Four children and thirteen grandchildren later I did return it. With interest!

Sharon and I started talking on the phone at first. After about a month we started dating. The first date we went on was to a Syracuse University basketball game. I thought I was honoring Sharon by taking her to see Dave Bing, my idol and the star of S.U.'s basketball team. I was a big basketball fan. I also spent thousands of hours on a basketball court where I developed my skills. Basketball was my primary interest after my parent's divorce.

My father and Lydia were in the front seat when we picked Sharon up. We sat in the back seat and Sharon thought I was extremely bold when I put my arm around her shoulders. We barely knew each other. She moved my arm off of her and put it back down. She was not impressed.

She had never dated before and thought I was moving too fast for a first date. I was the first and last. The Lord saved her only for me. She has never kissed anybody else other than me.

I had been raised in a Pentecostal church.

THE EARLY YEARS

Not to criticize anybody, but I felt like when Sharon and I started getting to know each other that she was the first real Christian that ever entered my life. I had seen a lot of Sunday morning smiles and "praise the Lords" but I never saw the corresponding actions during the week that would indicate that it was anything but a religious experience. It wasn't really a "knowing God" experience.

Even my own grandmother, when my grandfather would come home drunk, would go from being a nice gal after a Sunday morning service to cussing him out. I thought, "Why is she forcing me to go to church when it isn't really affecting her language that much?"

Sharon was like a breath of fresh air. When I finally saw a genuine Christian, even though I wasn't one myself at that time, it drew me towards her and helped us bond. I could see the direction that this relationship was going.

We dated for a couple of years or so. We had a favorite hangout in Auburn called, "Eddie's Fish Fry." We were creatures of habit and would go to the same place pretty much all the time.

I was involved with two or three different basketball leagues that were in Auburn. Sharon would attend many of the games but she carried a magazine with her because she was bored.

I found out very quickly that God was teaching me humility. I was a star in that basketball league. I had developed my skills to a high level with thousands of hours of playing, so naturally I wanted to have my girlfriend appreciate it. The buzzer would go off at the end of the game and I would ask her: "How did we do tonight?" and she would say: "Oh is the game over?" So God was teaching me some humility before I even knew Him. I found out Sharon was reading a magazine while I was scoring 35 points.

I finally realized that we were growing more and more in love. Both of us were not familiar with dating. One evening I picked a side road fairly close to where she had gone to high school, and brought the engagement ring with me. We pulled down a side street and we sat there and talked and then I proposed. It wasn't very romantic and if I had it to do over again I would go to a restaurant and get a private candle-lit table. But she was very happy to put the ring on her hand and it is still on her hand to this day.

We got married on July 24th 1966. We moved in with my mother and two sisters so we could save money for a down payment on a home. Then our first child Sherry came along. After Sherry was born, Sharon felt that she should help out financially and so my mother and sisters watched the baby while Sharon worked the three-to-eleven shift as a nurse's aide. Sharon did that for four or five years.

I continued going to church but my heart wasn't really in it. I went to church because my grandmother and then my wife pressured me. If it were up to me I would have done something else.

I had been to countless church meetings and listened to thousands of "altar calls" to receive Christ, but I had never responded. I had watched my father (who was a member of our church) leave four defenseless children. I thought: *This stuff is not real. These church people never live what they say. They go to church and they sing, "Victory in Jesus," every Sunday, but they might as well be eating a dill pickle at the same time.*

They would sing the tremendous anthems of the church but I saw precious little victory in their lives. I thought if that's what serving Jesus is, I got more victory on the basketball court with my friends. That's real; this is just nothing but dead religion.

EXPLOITS IN THE MIRACULOUS

I just wasn't a person designed for dead religion. Looking back on it now I realize that I had to have more than religion. I knew the Bible and I could quote Bible verses. I had a good ability to memorize Bible verses. I learned them from the time I was a little boy. I knew the Bible almost as good as the ministers that were doing the preaching. All the salvation messages and altar calls didn't mean anything to me because I didn't see anything that I wanted to emulate. I thought: *I'm as good a person as those people are.* People hadn't impressed me and neither did their religion.

I hung out with the wrong crowd. I started going to bars with the other guys. I suppose I should have realized the Lord had a call on my life because while they were drinking all I ever ordered was a Diet Coke. I never drank alcohol. They would try to buy me drinks and I would say: "I don't want any of that slop you're drinking." If I had had an ounce of sense then I should have known that God was setting me apart for something. I had no friends at church my age because I didn't have any respect for anyone at church. I thought they were all just hypocrites.

I was in the worst of both worlds. I wasn't totally in the world. I didn't want to drink with them, but when they wanted to go somewhere I went along. At the same time I'm going to church, but I'm not in the youth group. I just didn't see anything in them that I wanted to emulate.

2

My Conversion

My Uncle Bert was pastor of a small Baptist church in Fredericksburg, Virginia. I had never actually met my Uncle Bert until the time that my grandfather started to get very sick (August of 1971). Uncle Bert was already well-known to me because I had heard stories about him.

I was told if he came in contact with you all he wanted to know was: One. Are you saved? Two. Are you exhibiting the fruit of the Holy Spirit in your life? That meant no more to me at the time than an apple or an orange. The expression "fruit of the Holy Spirit" was a foreign language to me. But Uncle Bert was big on checking your fruit. He was on assignment from God as a fruit inspector.

I never really wanted to meet Uncle Bert because he was legendary in my family. He had 11 brothers and he was constantly after them to get saved. Uncle Bert came to Syracuse because my grandfather was dying. About a week before my grandfather's death he entered into the room where grandfather was confined to a hospital bed. There were about 25 or more people packed into it.

Bert made the rounds, shaking hands with everyone and came up to me and said: "You must be young Steve that I've heard so much about." My grandmother had told him I was a "tremendous young man of God" because I always acted like a Christian in front of her. He came over to me and said, "How are you and the Lord doing? Is everything good between you and the Lord?" I said, "Oh it couldn't be better. The Lord and I are in great shape with each other." He said, "That's what I thought. That's what your grandmother told me." He gave me a hug and kept on going. And I thought: *God, if you are up there, thank you for letting this wild man pass by me.* I didn't want him to get me dropping to my knees in front of 25 members of my family. I would have lied to him and gone through a prayer that I didn't mean. Uncle Bert stayed there for a day or two and spent time with my grandfather.

The big turning point of my life was after

everybody had left and things were becoming somewhat normal again. My grandfather called me into his room. He was more like a father to me than a grandfather. Other than my wife, he was also my closest friend in the world. He called me over and said, "Pull up a chair." He was a forceful man. He and his brothers were strong and built like giants. They worked in the coal mines of Altoona, Pennsylvania from the time they were ten years old. They had all grown up in the coal mines after quitting school at an early age. They came from a poor family of all coal miners. So they were rough and tough take-charge type of guys. When my grandfather came to Syracuse he worked for 27 years as a supervisor and foreman of the Globe Forge Steel Company on Erie Blvd.

When he called me into his room and told me to pull up a chair he said, "Give me your hand." He didn't ask me, he just told me. My grandfather would just bark orders. He was just that type of a guy. He would scare strangers but once they got to know him he had the heart of a pussycat, but with a gruff exterior.

He took my hand and said, "I'm going to be dying in about a week or so."

By this time he had been saved for about the

last five years. He led a rough life up until then. Before salvation he and my other grandfather were pretty good drinkers on the weekend and he didn't care too much about the Lord. After grandfather accepted Christ he was consistently going to church. He loved the Lord.

"I know you are running from the Lord and I want to lead you in a prayer to dedicate yourself to the Lord because I know you're not ready to meet him. Should you die right now, I know where you are going just by your lifestyle. You are fooling your grandmother but you're not fooling me. Even though I see you going to church, I know everything is not right between you and the Lord. I don't want to go to my grave knowing that you are going to be lost."

Nothing, other than my parent's divorce, was as traumatic in my life as him asking me to pray with him. I couldn't lie to this man because I loved him too much. I began to weep and he asked, "What's wrong?" I answered, "I can't pray this prayer with you because I don't want you to die and leave this earth thinking I did something to deceive you. I've never tried to deceive you. I have always respected you and I'm not going to pray a prayer that I don't mean now. I'm not ready to make this commitment to the Lord." I was just crying my eyes out as I talked to him.

So he said, "Is that your final decision?"

"Yes, it is."

"Well, get out of your chair and lean over here and give me a hug."

So I did and he gave me a bear hug I thought would break both of our hearts.

Then he said, "I don't know when I'll have a chance to hug you again. I need to hug you. I love you, but I won't see you again because I'm going to heaven and you've charted a course for yourself that is going to take you to hell. I want to at least show you that I love you. The fact that we have made different decisions for our lives…I'm hurting that you don't want to get saved…but that's your choice. In the after life I'm probably never going to see you again."

When he said that it was just like somebody took a knife and just threw it right through my heart. I couldn't have felt any worse if somebody had beaten me with a baseball bat. It just knocked the life right out of me.

I wanted so badly to please him. He had been so wonderful to pick up the pieces for me and be a father figure for me. He took me everywhere and did everything with me. But I couldn't lie to him.

Sure enough a week later he went to be with the Lord and I never would get another opportunity to pray with him.

After his death Sharon said to me, "You know the family is going to be coming in from all over the country. We have to start making the arrangements for the wake and the funeral." I got very upset with her. I said, "Sharon, unless you want a war between you and I, don't ask me again to be at his wake. I horribly disappointed this man by not granting his last request. There's no way I can stand in front of his casket. I would go to pieces. You are going to have to take Sherry and go to the wake and funeral yourself. I'm going to have to pass on this one. I can't see this man lying there dead. I just can't face him. I can't do it."

Instead of arguing with me, like a lot of women would do, she just said, "I'll be praying for you, Steve."

I told her, "Don't even tell me that. Don't be praying for me. I don't want you praying for me because if you pray God may answer your prayers and make it so I will go and I don't want to go there."

I was so broken hearted that I had failed him.

MY CONVERSION

The man had treated me so wonderfully. I would feel like a hypocrite being there to see him. I was haunted by the fact that now he was dead and I had no chance to ever take his hand and pray.

So the day of the wake came along and Sharon hadn't bothered me since. Then a few hours before it was time to go to the afternoon viewing hours she said: "Honey, you're going to have to take a shower and get ready. We have to be there soon."

I snapped at her, "I'm not going. I'm *not* going." She did the smart thing and just left me alone. God must have been working on my heart because soon I started feeling a peace and I eventually got ready and we went.

We went to the afternoon wake and then in the evening our good friends Joanne and Artie were nice enough to watch our daughter Sherry. She was only about four and we didn't feel like it was appropriate to take her, even though my grandfather loved her tremendously. What a close relationship he had with her. We dropped Sherry off at their home and then Sharon and I went on to the funeral home. Soon after we arrived I walked up to the casket with Sharon and a group of other people. Later I walked up by myself and stood looking at him. It was like his last words just started to haunt me: "Give me a hug. I'll never see you again."

I couldn't stand it. I just couldn't stand it. I didn't know what it was then, but I was under the convicting power of the Holy Spirit. I said to Sharon, "I'll be back to pick you up but I've got to go do some thinking." I ran out of the funeral home and began walking up and down a six or seven block area.

I was so distraught. I just thought my life wasn't even worth living. Other than my wife, I'd lost the best friend I've ever had. I was really, really hurting over it. Looking back on it, as I was pacing that night, I know the Lord was speaking to me: "Be at peace. Be at peace. I've got a plan for you."

I just shrugged that off and said, "Leave me alone. I've got enough problems right now. Don't bother me now. Of all the times for you to talk to me this is not a good time."

I wasn't receiving the peace of God. He was offering it to me but I wasn't receiving it. But at some point before I came back from that walk He had softened me up. I returned to the funeral home and stood in front of my grandfather's casket. Without praying out loud I said in my heart, "God I know you are talking to me. Just help me through this time."

MY CONVERSION

I still didn't ask to be saved but at least I started reaching out to Him for the first time. Soon it was time to leave. Sharon and I left and we headed back to Artie and Joanne's house to pick up our daughter Sherry. Normally when Joanne would babysit for us, Sharon and I would pull up in the driveway and Sharon would go and get Sherry. This time God had a different plan.

Joanne came out and started talking to Sharon on her side of the car and I said: "Well, if you two are talking I'll run in and get the baby."

As I entered the house the only light that was on was just a little light where Sherry was sleeping in the living room. I walked through the kitchen and turned a corner through an open arch into the living room. I entered the room and I took about two steps and it was just like the Holy Spirit froze my body. I mean that literally. I could not move. Then an audible voice spoke to me and said: "Give your life to Jesus, right now. Your running is over."

Such a presence of God overwhelmed me that I knew it was now or never. I knew this was my moment of decision. It was either going to happen now or, in all likelihood, it would never happen. My heart had been prepared and softened by all that had happened during the past week.

I looked up at that ceiling and I said, "God, I don't even know why you want me. I'm worthless. I'm like a piece of trash. I don't know why you would want to bother with me, but if you are real I want to live a life like the one I see my wife living. But I'm powerless to change myself. I'm just not a good guy, but Jesus if you are real come into my life and change me."

Immediately when I said that it was like a heavenly hook came down into my belly and down into my body. I could feel something grab onto all the worthlessness and the rejection I had felt. It was like a piece of machinery was latching onto it and just pulling it up through my chest area and right up through my face. I could literally feel it being expelled out of the top of my head. When it left my body, I felt like the most pure human being. One moment I felt like a piece of trash and the next I felt like I was 20 feet tall. I felt as pure as the freshly fallen snow.

I heard the Lord speak to my heart, "You are of worth to me and I will take your grandfather's place. I will take up where he left off. He's gone now but I won't ever forsake you. I'm here now. Trust me to be more than you had before. I'll be more than what your grandfather was to you."

I knew for the first time in my life I was not a hypocrite any more. I knew I had started on a journey. I had no idea where it was taking me but I knew I was on the right path.

I just glided over to my daughter and I picked her up. I had a new bounce in my step as I walked out to the car. Sharon took Sherry and put her in the seat. When we got back to my mother's home Sharon looked at me and said, "You did it, didn't you?"

It's hard for a man to humble himself in front of a woman and so I played macho a little bit:

"I did what?"

She said: "You know what."

Then I felt that it was going to be all right to tell her. "Yeah. You mean, did I give my life to the Lord?"

"Yes."

So I asked, "How did you know?"

"You're glowing. You are glowing like a light bulb with the glory of God. Steve, I knew it when you got in the car and got behind that wheel. I knew you had given your life to the Lord. I had prayed so hard for you to do it. It finally happened."

EXPLOITS IN THE MIRACULOUS

Our son was born a month after my grandfather's funeral. My grandfather had told Sharon: "I won't live to see it but in a few weeks you are going to have a son this time." He prophesied to Sharon that it would be a boy and sure enough when the baby was born it was our one and only son. We named him after my grandfather.

3

Early Lessons

Seed Time and Harvest

The Bible says in Matthew 6:21: *"For where your treasure is, there will your heart be also."* So it shouldn't be surprising that if you want to be a man or woman of God, you are going to have to let God put His finger on your treasure so He can get at your heart.

In the summer of 1971, Sharon and I were in the process of saving up for a down payment on our first home. We were still very early in our marriage. My father and Lydia had heard that Jack Van Impe was coming to Auburn Community College. He wasn't as well known then as he is today. He was coming for five nights of meetings. That immediately piqued my interest because I had a number of his books, so I asked my father if we could go along with them to the meetings. We went all five nights. I was just amazed. I saw why Dr. Van Impe has the nickname of: "The Walking Bible."

Dr. Van Impe said that he had a prayer request that he would like to throw out to us while he was there. He wanted us to come into agreement with him that the Lord would provide $5,000. He explained the contracts were ready for his signature for him to be broadcast on the radio all over the nation of Russia. He was $5,000 short to do that.

He preached a fine message that night and when the service was over and we were in the back seat of my dad's car going home, the Holy Spirit started to speak to me. Sharon and I had already saved about $18,000, but we needed more, or the bank wouldn't give us a loan, since we had no credit.

I heard the Holy Spirit speak so clearly it was like it was an audible voice. He said, "When you go to the service tomorrow night take a check for $5,000 and give it to Jack Van Impe so he can get on the radio in Russia." That was probably the first time I ever heard the voice of the Lord as clearly as that. I can look back at it and say that's where I first began to develop the art of hearing His voice.

EARLY LESSONS

So I leaned over to Sharon. I didn't want my father to hear me so I whispered it to her. She said we would talk about it when we got back to my mother's home. So when we got back we went into our bedroom and talked about it. She said, "Steve as long as you know that was the Lord, by all means go ahead and do it, but if you have any doubt, that's a lot of money and it will set us back quite a ways from being able to get that home."

Five thousand dollars was a lot of money in 1971 and it took us a long time to save it. Living with her mother-in-law, Sharon really wanted to get out and have her own home, but I knew I had heard from God. So the next day I told her again, "I've got to do it." So she gave her consent.

During the course of my workday, I went and got a cashier's check for Dr. Van Impe for the $5,000. That night we went back and he made the same appeal: "Are you praying and believing with me? I've got to get on the radio in Russia."

The service ended and the Lord said to me not to put the offering in the plate. "I want you to give it to him personally." Again I heard that voice of the Holy Spirit speak to me. So I kept the check in my sport jacket pocket and when the service ended, I told my father and stepmother that I needed to talk to Jack Van Impe. I let the place pretty much empty out and walked up onto the platform.

He asked me "What's your name young man?" I told him my name. He said nice to meet you, and the next words out of his mouth you think would have been "How did you enjoy the service?" or something like that but instead he looked me right in the eye and said, "Steve, do you think the last couple of nights the people have sensed the urgency of how badly I need this $5,000 to get on the radio in Russia?" I was only 27 years old at the time. I knew he did not expect the money to be coming from me. I said, "Dr. Van Impe, I have no idea what the other people sensed, but I got the urgency of it. I've got something for you." I opened up my jacket and handed him the check for $5,000. He thanked me that we were willing to make the contribution.

The Lord planted deep in my spirit what a joy it was to give. It just really made us feel like we had done something good for the kingdom of God.

Soon after that we were in a church meeting. There was a missionary lady attending that evening stationed way up in Canada in the Hudson Bay area. On a Wednesday night I would never have more than 10 or 15 dollars in my wallet. I just didn't walk around carrying money, but I happened to have three $50 bills with me that night. I looked over at Sister Carter during the service and the Holy Spirit said, "Have Sharon give her the $150." So I heard again clearly. I was beginning to be able to hear from the Holy Spirit. Once you listen to him and obey He is more than willing to talk to you more and more.

Sharon said, "Why don't you give this to her?" I said, "No, the Lord told me to have you give it to her."

Sharon went over and gave her a "Pentecostal handshake" and put it in her hand.

She gave Sharon a big hug and stuck it in her purse without looking at it.

Nobody looks at money when you give it to them. They don't want to embarrass you or themselves.

The next evening when I came home from work Sharon said she had an interesting story to tell me.

"You know that money you had me give Sister Carter last night? She called me about 10:30 this morning. The two tires on the front of her old car were completely bald. She had to make another long trip up into Canada and then go by canoe all by herself to reach Hudson Bay to minister to some remote tribe up there. She had applied for a Sunoco Credit Card three weeks ago because she had to buy tires. She called and told me she had already priced those tires. With tax and all they came to just under $150. She said we saved her mission trip to Canada because the credit card is not coming in the mail in time to use it, plus she couldn't afford to go into debt anyway."

God is a giver and since we have him in our heart that makes us want to give too.

I heard a wisdom key from a TV evangelist that I've found to be true: "Nothing leaves heaven until something leaves your hand.' The Lord replaced the $5,000 and Sharon and I now had the down payment on our home. We didn't live with my mother much longer after that because the Lord blessed us in phenomenal ways. He wanted us to have a home. We soon bought our starter home, a three-bedroom ranch house.

God then took me from manual labor putting on roofing and siding to being over sales in our own family construction business. Within 10 years we were able to sell our little starter home for a $23,000 profit and move into a four bedroom colonial home.

EARLY LESSONS

One thing I preach about everywhere I go: Don't think if you are giving 10% of your gross pay as a tithe that you are a giver. You haven't even reached a level of real giving yet. You are only paying back God what is already His. That's not even a gift. That would be like if I said to you on a Monday, "Can I borrow $50 from you to get me through until Friday when I cash my paycheck?" You say "yes" and hand it to me. When I catch up to you on Friday evening and I pay you back the $50 can I say I gave you a gift today? No. I gave you back your own $50. So a tithe isn't even *giving* at all. Offerings are gifts that get God's attention. We can't even get most Christians to the level of paying their tithes and they wonder why God can't bless them.

When the Bible says: "give and it shall be given, pressed down shaken together" it's not talking about the tithes because you aren't giving yet. That's just giving back to God what's His. A lot of people that are paying tithes are not seeing a big harvest because they have not really given anything. They can't get the "pressed down shaken together and running over" until they get beyond the tithes.

The Beginning of Miracles

Our daughter Sarah was three and a half years old when we were getting ready for church one Sunday morning. I was dressed up in a white shirt and my black suit. Sarah stuck her three fingers in the doorjamb of her brother's bedroom. He didn't know she was there and wanted privacy so he slammed the door. It cut her fingers very deeply. Sharon had been a nurse's aide so she was able to get one finger to stop bleeding but she said the other two were each going to need several stitches. She couldn't get them to stop bleeding. Sharon said: "We are going to have to get her to the hospital right away."

Little Sarah was hysterical and blood was spattering all over. Sharon said to just grab her and let's pray for her. Because of the pain her body was quaking uncontrollably as I put her on my lap.

This was really our first adventure in the miraculous as a husband and wife team. God was about to break loose in our life. He was putting something on us and on me in particular. As I held her on my lap I put my hand over the bleeding hand, Sharon put her hand on mine and the two older children put their hands on ours. We made a pyramid of hands. Blood was just pouring all over. I closed my eyes and said a very simple prayer. It was a real "theological" prayer: "HELP!" That's all I knew at the time. To our amazement when we took our hands off there wasn't even a hint that she had been in an accident. The Lord had healed the three fingers. You couldn't even tell they had been hurt. There was no blood. There were no cuts. I immediately looked down at my white shirt that I knew had been covered with blood. There was no blood. There was no blood on Sarah at all. We retraced all of our steps up and down the entire hallway where she had been running and bleeding on the floor and walls. We had watched her do it. It was like the Lord had rewound a video of the accident and made it go away. It was as if it had never happened. We knew we were into the "real deal" of God's miracle power. All of us were just totally amazed. We realized that we had seen a miracle of biblical proportions.

When Sarah was healed it wasn't by the prayer of a man of faith. It was more like a prayer of a drowning man screaming, "Throw me a rope!" I was just a desperate father. All I was asking was for God to clot the bleeding so we could get her to proper medical treatment. I never would have thought that when we took our hands off there would be three perfectly healed fingers and no blood anywhere in the house.

I thought if God could do that with no faith involved on my part at all, what could He do if someone mixed some faith in with these things? I started to think about further down the line. What if I can get myself to the place where I could really be a man of faith? What could God do then? This was the beginning of our seeing miracles. I had a deep feeling that God would somehow take us on to further adventures.

I began to grow in faith after I got more knowledge on the subject. I started to read literature on faith and devoured everything I could from Kenneth Hagin's teaching. I studied his videos and books. I also sat under his ministry in person six different times. A lot of people consider him the father of the faith movement. I learned a lot about the miraculous from Brother Hagin's books and being in his meetings. Faith "cometh by hearing, and hearing by the word of God" (Romans 10:17 KJV). Kenneth Hagin was an expert in that area and the more I learned, the more I got excited about doing it myself.

4

Door to Door
with George

The Assembly of God church we attended in Syracuse began a door-to-door visitation program to reach the lost. The program was very successful. We eventually had over 40 teams of people going out by two's every Thursday evening. The church grew from 300 members to over 1000.

I was eventually paired with a man named George. It was like a pilot, co-pilot program. George, being the experienced visitation worker, was the pilot. I was what they called the co-pilot, meaning I was to be trained by watching him before I would attempt to do it myself.

George was only a couple years older than I but he was an expert at one-on-one evangelism. That was his gift. He was quite tall, about 6'2" with a slender build, brown eyes and hair, and a very winsome personality.

From 1975 through 1978 we went on visitation together every Thursday night. One night the program director assigned us to a name on a card in the inner city of Syracuse. He said, "I'd like you guys to go visit this young man here. He hasn't been to church for a while."

Sometimes we were assigned to a person and sometimes we went cold canvassing door to door. This night the director assigned us to go to a house on Onondaga Street. It turned out to be a group home for young men. Our intention was to go there for one night to visit one person but God had other plans.

The home housed 25 troubled young men. Our assignment was to go one evening for two hours, but within eight and a half months we had led everybody in the building and 27 of their friends to the Lord. They came from all over the city because of the power of God that was in that place.

When George and I originally went to visit the guy on the contact card it turned out he didn't even live there any more. The manager of the house was a man named Peter. George said to him, "As long as we are here can we come in and talk to some of your young men about the Lord?" Peter said, "I suppose so, I don't think that will hurt." So we went in and struck a pretty good rapport with the men and started doing Bible studies. We saw miracle after miracle, but the greatest one was Tiny.

Tiny got that nickname because he was about 6'3" and about 250 pounds of solid muscle. As he grew older, he rode with the Hell's Angel's motorcycle gang in California. He had killed a young man down south and served time for second-degree murder. Anything you can think of that was bad Tiny had managed to fall into.

Every week we would bring a big sheet pizza and three two-liter bottles of soda. George knew it was better to first spend 20 to 25 minutes socializing with the guys than to just cram Jesus down their throats.

Tiny wanted nothing to do with me and George. For months he never came into the Bible study. Tiny wouldn't even eat any pizza with us. He stayed in the TV room next to where we met. We would invite him in and he would say, "No. No. Just leave me alone." But he couldn't deny the presence of the Lord because every week people were getting saved.

We found out Tiny had been really hurt. He

had been given away. When he was two weeks old he was placed in a basket at the door of an orphanage by his parents and just abandoned there. At least they had the decency to wait in a car across the street until somebody came and answered the door. His parents exited his life, never intending to see him again. They just didn't want him.

After nearly eight months, George announced to the group that we could not keep coming there forever. We have to move on and do other things with our visitation program. He informed the group we were going to be there three more weeks and then we would be finished. On the way out that night we had to walk right past the TV room where Tiny was watching TV with a couple of his buddies. All of a sudden I feel this hand reach out from behind and grab me. It was Tiny.

I was shocked. He said, "I've got to talk to you and George. I've got to talk to you right now." I said "fine" and I told George that Tiny wanted to talk to us.

Tiny said, No. Not here in the TV room. Come into my room."

He took us to his bedroom and he propped himself up against the headboard of his bed. We pulled up a couple of chairs next to him. He told us the story of his life and how his parents abandoned him and how he was in the Hell's Angels gang, the murder and so on. We found out even though Tiny had not been in the Bible study group, the Holy Spirit, a little at a time, had been getting his attention. When we announced that we were only staying three more weeks Tiny felt he had to make a move towards God now or it was going to be all over for the rest of his life. So he started to cry. Tiny was 25 years old and built like a tank and all of a sudden this big husky guy began to weep and unveil one horror story after another.

He said, "This God you guys talk about… how is it that He made me to be abandoned when I was just two weeks old? Did I deserve that? Even worse, eight years ago I was involved in an awful car accident. The only thing holding me together is a stainless steel rod running down my back and into my hip area. If I get into a squatting position I can never get up without help. This loving God that I hear you guys talking about, couldn't He have at least kept me from having a stainless steel rod? Why can't I just walk normal and have a normal body?"

He went on telling us things like that. George was very compassionate and a "power-house" of a man of God. So George said, "Why don't we take it one step at a time Tiny? Number one, you need to be saved. You understand that. You have heard enough about what is going on here." And George took his hand and said, "Take my hand and pray with me." There was one thing about George. When he was working at his gift of one-on-one evangelism you couldn't say "no" to him.

Tiny was sitting on the bed and George took his hand and as George led him in a sinner's prayer, it was just like in the movie *The Exorcist*. Tiny went from a sitting position and was literally thrown like a rag doll on the bed. This was a big guy and he was flopping like a rag doll. I honestly thought the bed was going to break.

The Lord was giving him the whole package. George's hand had the power of God on it. It was like touching an electric wire and getting a shock. So Tiny is flopping all over the bed and he's saying the sinner's prayer, he's crying, being filled with the Holy Spirit, speaking in a heavenly language and getting healed of this steel rod all at one time. The work was all done in a matter of 3 or 4 minutes.

Finally Tiny said, "What happened to me? What did you do?"

He turned to George: "What did you do to me?"

George said, "We didn't do anything. We just introduced you to Jesus. Stand up. Get down in that squatting position right now."

Tiny asked us if we would help him get back up.

George told him "We won't help you."

"Why would I get down in that squatting position?"

George said, "Just do what I tell you."

He got down and all of a sudden he realized he could get back up. George had him doing it again, faster and faster and faster. Tiny was more ecstatic than any man I had seen in my life. But after awhile Tiny sat back down on the edge of the bed and started to weep.

He said, "Steve. George. There is one other thing that you guys could do for me. I look like a big macho guy but I've been hurt so bad that my parents gave me away. Hurt far more than this steel rod I got healed from. I won't ever be fully healed unless I can meet my real birth parents and ask them why they gave me away and sent me into this life of hell for 25 years. I need to know if your God can perform a miracle and get me to see my parents before my life is over."

George said, "Get up off of that bed right

now Tiny. Just stand in a circle with us. I thought you were going to ask us something hard. That's nothing. What do you think that is to God? That doesn't even reach the level of being difficult. That's a piece of cake. Steve, let's hold hands with him."

So I'm looking at George and to be honest I thought the man had lost his mind. I thought he just finally flipped out.

So we held hands and George prayed, "Jesus you see what a simple thing this is for you to perform for Tiny. We thank you that Tiny's parents are going to meet with him very shortly and you are going to work this out so easy. It's going to be such a joy. What reconciliation there is going to be when they meet! We thank you right now that you heard this young man's prayer and we thank you that this is a done deal. Amen in Jesus' name."

George said, "They will be coming to get you, Tiny!"

Both of us gave Tiny a big hug welcoming him into the family of God.

We left and got out into my car, but before I started the motor up I said to George, "I believe in the power of God in the area of healings. I have no problem for that. Leading him to the Lord, that wasn't a problem. The baptism of the Holy Spirit, we saw that happen many times. But don't you think you went a little out of your authority to speak for God? Those parents could be dead, they could be living on the other end of the earth, they could be in Australia or one of them could be remarried. There are so many variables here with this thing, I think you went overboard."

We had become very intimate friends so I felt free to tell him that he went over the edge on this one. George replied that the Holy Spirit told him to tell Tiny those things.

I said, "Are you sure of that?"

George said, "You'll see. Start the car up and let's go home."

He was just as calm as could be. This didn't fluster him at all. This was a mighty man of faith. I learned a lot from him. I learned from everybody God put in my path. That's how you become a man or woman of God. You take a piece from each person that God puts you with.

The following week we returned to the group home for the next-to-the-last Bible study. Tiny attended the Bible study for the first time. He was one of the first ones there and gave George and I a big bear hug.

The next week, however, at the final Bible study everybody was there except Tiny. I said, "We can't start, Tiny is not here." The director, Peter, said that Tiny was gone. George said, "We can see that. Did he go down to the corner store to get a bottle of Coke or something?"

Peter explained that two days before there was a knock at the front door. It was a married couple. They told Peter they had abandoned their baby boy 25 years before. Three weeks back neither one of them could sleep. They tossed and turned until both of them were worn out physically. They could not get a moment's peace. (From the time George and I had prayed with Tiny.) One morning they finally compared notes with each other. The husband said, "I'm under terrible conviction from God for what we did with that baby boy of ours." She said she was too. "We've got to make this right if it is at all possible." Somehow the Lord led them to the proper agencies that tracked him to the group home.

Peter had the parents wait inside and went and told Tiny that there were some people there that wanted to talk with him. Peter led them into Tiny's room. The parents dropped down on their knees and with tears in their eyes they begged his forgiveness. Tiny immediately and graciously forgave them. There was a beautiful reconciliation.

It turned out his parents had lived all along just 72 miles north in Watertown, NY. They asked Tiny to please come "pick up the pieces," live with them, and be their son. That was why Tiny wasn't at the Bible study. He was home with his parents.

Later that night George and I stopped at a restaurant. I reminded George how I thought he had really missed it and was off the wall in telling Tiny he was going to reconcile with his parents. Now it had come to pass. I wanted to know how George was so sure. How could he hear so clearly from heaven?

George said, "Haven't you noticed every single time that we have gone out for four years that we get people saved...every Thursday night with no exceptions?"

I said, "Yes, I noticed that."

George continued, "Haven't you seen the amount of miracles that we have been allowed to do in Jesus' name?" I told him that I saw the Lord use us to perform them but that I didn't understand how they were happening for us and not happening for most of the other visitation teams.

He explained, "I never wanted to tell you this. I

wanted it to be just between the Lord and me. But for the last four years I have not eaten breakfast, lunch, or dinner on the Thursdays we go on visitation. It hasn't been me. The Lord has not allowed food to touch my lips. The Lord also led me to be in an attitude of worship all that day on my job. I don't do it out loud and look like a fanatic where I work, but I am in an attitude of praise and worship to God all day long. I'm constantly building up my spirit man so that when we go out that night I am able to receive the direction from God that He gives us to do. Learn that lesson. Always be in an attitude of submission to the Lord. It isn't just a Sunday morning or a church meeting thing. Have that become a lifestyle and you can become a tremendous man of God."

5

On the Job with God

Being the salesman for our family construction company put me in constant contact with the public. I had to meet people of all kinds of backgrounds and nationalities—older people, younger people, and people from every walk of life. I wasn't ashamed to let these people know that this was a God centered company. I wasn't using religion as a way to close the sale. I was taking care of their construction needs, but I also wanted to help with their physical and spiritual needs.

Sometimes I would talk to them about the Lord and the things of God in such depth that I would have to reset the appointment for another day.

To me the evangelist part of me was more important than the businessman part. It was like I had a ministry inside of a business.

An example of this is the story of Marty and Betty Jones in North Syracuse. Betty went to Syracuse Baptist church. She was a wonderful gal. She was saved but her husband and the grown daughter who lived with them weren't. They were repeat customers. We did four or five jobs for them over the time we were in business. Every two or three years they would call us back to do the next project.

Early on I would talk to Marty about his condition with the Lord and he would say, "I don't really believe in that stuff like you and my wife do." I didn't push him the first couple of jobs but after we got to know each other a little more I spoke freely with him.

After I had a business relationship with them for about 10 or 12 years, Betty took me aside one day and said, "Steve, our daughter is very, very sick. She's got something that the doctors can't solve. Even though she is not a Christian she is open for you to come some night and minister to her. If I can get Marty to allow you to come back some evening when you are off work, would you come and pray for our daughter?"

I asked her, "Will this get Marty upset?"

"I'll let you know. Let me talk to him."

So she talked to Marty and he told her that it would be okay. I came back that night. Marty was close to 70 years old. Their daughter was in her forties. So I gave the daughter a little teaching about how I was going to pray for her and I said, "Stand here in the center of the room. I'm not the healer. I'm just going to lay my hand lightly on your head and just command this disease to leave your body." I said, "Marty, I'm going to need you to catch." He said, "You're going to need me to what?" Now I realized that this man never went to any church. Catch? He probably thought we were going to play some kind of game.

I stood him behind her.

He asked, "What's going to happen to my daughter?"

I said, "She is probably going to fall under the power of the Lord when He heals her."

He asked me what that meant and I told him.

He replied, "That kind of stuff doesn't happen."

"It could so you better be ready for it."

So, I went after that disease and commanded it to go and boom...she fell right back. He had to catch her and lay her on the ground. He looked at Betty and he said, "Honey, what in the world was it that Steve just did to her? What in the world is that? What happened to her? What did you do to her?"

I said, "I didn't do anything to her. She just had an encounter with Jesus. It's called falling out under the Spirit." She was healed.

Now boldness came on me. As Marty was sitting on the couch with his wife I said, "Marty you're a nice guy and I think the world of you. I think that the feeling is mutual. I don't think you would keep having us do all these jobs around here if you didn't think the same about me. Is that right?"

"Yeah, that's right."

"You know what Marty, I don't know if you believe in heaven or hell, but they are both real. Hell is filled with nice guys like you. Hell isn't filled with just all bad guys."

Marty asked, "Why would God send nice people to hell?"

"He doesn't. They just choose to go there on their own because they take the path that leads there instead of the path that leads to eternal life. Jesus said I am the way the truth and the life and any man that comes to Him can have eternal life. But you have to come to him. There are good guys that won't come to him. You don't go to heaven or hell because of how good you are. You go to heaven because you are saved. You are a nice guy but you're not saved. Therefore if you were to die right now, you are going to hell."

He said, "What do you mean I'm going to hell? I'm a nice guy."

"I just told you. The Bible says in Isaiah 64:6 that 'all our righteousnesses are as filthy rags.' You are a nice guy but in God's sight you are like a filthy rag."

"Boy that's a tough thing to tell me when you call me your friend."

I said, "I am your friend. That's why I'm being honest with you. The goodness of Marty compared to the glory of God is like a dirty filthy rag."

After I explained the plan of salvation to him I asked, "Would you like to receive Jesus now?"

"Well, you tell me if I don't, I'm going to hell. Right, Steve?"

"That's what I'm telling you. But I don't want you to get saved just to escape hell. I want you to get to spend the rest of your years going with your wife to church and growing in your relationship with Jesus."

He looked at her and he said, "Boy, Honey, he's making this sound urgent. I'm not getting any younger." Then he said, "What do I have to do to do this?"

"Just sit right there and hold your wife's hand. I'm going to kneel right in front of you and lead in the sinner's prayer."

So I led him to the Lord in a couple of minutes and he looked at his wife and he said, "Wow! I feel so clean. I feel so different. If I had known it was that simple I would have done that a long, long time ago."

"You've done it now. Jesus is very pleased with you and the angels in heaven are rejoicing."

You need to understand that his wife was a Baptist woman. She didn't believe in the Baptism of the Holy Spirit with the evidence of speaking in tongues.

I said, "Marty I would like to do one other thing for you before I leave."

"What's that?"

"Now that you are saved you need to be filled with the Holy Spirit with the evidence of speaking in tongues."

"What in the world is that?"

I figure we've gone this far I might as well finish the job. I used an analogy that I thought they would understand. He had just received Jesus and he had the Holy Sprit in him but it was like a glass that was half filled with water. It wasn't overflowing. God wants the glass to be overflowing to other people.

Then Marty asked, "What about this speaking in tongues?"

"When I lay hands on you the Holy Spirit will really come on you. When you feel this heavenly language come, you do the speaking. God's going to give you this new language but he is a gentleman. He's not going to force you to speak it out. Just speak out loud what He gives you to say."

"Should I do this, Steve?"

"Yes, you should. It will give you power for serving the Lord."

"You didn't lie to me about the other thing. I know how good I feel now. What do I have to do to receive this?"

"Just stand up in the middle of the room."

So I got his daughter and Betty behind to catch him, laid my hand on him and said, "Holy Spirit, baptize him right now." Boom! Down he went on the floor and he was speaking in other tongues.

As he was lying on the floor he said to Betty, "Wow, honey this is phenomenal. What an experience!"

Now I turn my attention to Betty. I told her she needed the same thing and she agreed.

I said to Marty, "Let me pick you up now and we are going to do something different." He was glowing like a light bulb.

"Betty, you face your husband and I am going to catch you myself."

She said, "You're going to catch me? Who's going to pray for me?"

"Marty is going to pray for you. He's got the Holy Spirit now."

"I do?'

"Yes, you do!"

"What do you want me to do?"

I said, "Nothing. Just lay hands on her and say: 'Jesus, fill my wife right now with your Spirit.'"

He said, "Steve, you know how to do this stuff, but this is scaring me a little bit. I can't do this."

"You are right, but the Holy Spirit in you can. Just do what I'm telling you."

He touched her and…boom…she went down. His eyes got the size of dinner plates. The Lord came on them and did a tremendous work in them. They were both speaking in other tongues and praising God.

So now, we picked her up and I sat them down

on the couch. The daughter and I are in a couple of chairs on the other side of the room. I said, "How did you guys like that experience? They were still half out of it. Marty said, "Wow! I never experienced anything like this in my life!" Betty said, "This stuff doesn't happen in my church!"

I asked them, "Would you like another shot of the power of God?"

"How do we do that?"

"Just stand up right where you are." I was about 12 feet away from them.

"You ready, Betty?"

"Yes, I'm ready."

"You ready, Marty?"

"Yes. Are you coming over to touch me?"

"No. I don't have to touch you."

I just waved my hand at them. The Holy Spirit knocked them right back on the couch.

These were the kinds of things God did over the years on my job. I saw countless healings take place: People were healed of Carpal Tunnel Syndrome, bad backs, breathing problems, and lameness to name a few. Over the decades I visited tens of thousands of homes. So many people got saved or healed it led to getting phone calls like this:

"Hi, Steve. This is Jim Smith on Elm Street. Do you remember me? You did my bathroom. My brother-in-law is dying of lung cancer at the hospital. I thought about you and I knew I could call you at your office. Could you come and pray for him?"

That led me to being busy going to hospitals. Most nights I would drift in after 9 at night. Sharon would say to me, "Well, your supper is cold. You must have been talking about Jesus again!"

The Boy with the Sloping Eye

Just a little before my dad passed away in 1993 I was on an appointment connected with our construction company. It was at the house of an older woman about a mile or two from our home. Her daughter had just moved in along with her three children. Her daughter's marriage had busted up back in Ireland because her husband was a drunkard and not a very nice man. I was told she could not go back as he was abusive. The house was not big enough to accommodate all of them so they called our company to remodel the backroom into another bedroom.

ON THE JOB WITH GOD

When I was there I noticed this little boy walking around with a patch over his left eye. His mother wasn't there but the grandmother was. I wasn't paying too much attention to him as I was there conducting business with his grandmother and I signed a contract with her. I was picking up my briefcase to leave and I was almost to the door when I heard the Spirit of God say to me: "Leave your briefcase there and go sit at the table with the grandmother and ask her what's wrong with the little boy. Then ask if you can pray for him."

So I went back to her and I said: "Excuse me, the Lord just spoke to me. I've got to do something for your little grandson before I leave. What is wrong with his eye?" She said at birth, instead of both of his eyes being horizontal in his head like a normal child, his left eye was slanted at a forty-five degree angle and tipped in his head. (I can't remember what she said the medical term was. It was a mile long!) There was nothing any eye doctor or surgeon could do for him. All they could do was what they were doing.

About three times a year, the eye would fill with pus and they would have to take him to the doctor to have something put in it. Then they would put the patch on and leave it on for a week or so. Then they returned to the doctor to have the eye cleaned out. They had been doing that since he was born. He was now about four and a half years old.

I asked her, "Can I pray for him?" She said sure. I also asked if she would like to get involved in this prayer. I said: "Take my hand and we'll hold hands and you put your hand on his shoulder. If you don't mind I'll put my hand over the patch." She said that would be wonderful and thanked me for caring about him.

I just basically prayed a prayer like this saying: "Father God, we just come to you right now in Jesus' name, and Jesus, by the power of the Holy Spirit of God that resides in me, a believer, I just ask your healing anointing to flow through this hand of mine right now and bring total healing in this little boy's eye."

I didn't feel anything. You know sometimes you can feel the anointing go right out of your hand into a person and sometimes you don't. But you don't go by feelings. You go by faith. I just moved in faith and obedience to the voice of the Lord. I put him down off my lap and thanked her for the opportunity to pray for him and just went about my business. I really didn't think much more of it.

The next visit my father went back with me

to her home to get a material list for the crew. As soon as I knocked on the door, the grandmother went right by me like I wasn't even there and she said to my father: "Mr. Buza, Mr. Buza. Come in here. I've got to tell you an incredible story!" She told the story of what happened when I prayed for the boy. I knew from the enthusiasm in her voice that something very, very unusual had happened here.

She told my father that four or five days after we prayed, she and her daughter took Jimmy back to the eye doctor. As usual, he was set in an examination chair so a nurse could take off the patch and get ready for the doctor. This time when the nurse took off the patch she went running hysterically out of the room yelling at the top of her lungs, "Doctor! Doctor! Come in here! You have to drop what you are doing and come in here right now. Come see this."

When the doctor came in, the little boy's eye was totally straight in his head. No pus. No disease. The doctor had two other surgeons document this miracle. The three doctors certified that this was a flat out miracle of God. They told the mother and grandmother, "We can't explain this other than to say that you got a miracle from God. There is no other way this eye could be turned straight in his head. It isn't possible without Divine intervention. You ladies need to be very thankful that a higher power has intervened and touched your grandson." The doctors said it was the greatest miracle they had ever witnessed.

I asked the grandmother if I could hold Jimmy on my lap again. I got him on my lap and pulled him up so I could look at him eyeball to eyeball. I asked the grandmother to remind me which eye it was. They were both so perfect I couldn't even remember. I was just thrilled.

I was so excited that I went out of that house saying "Lord send me." From that point on I had a special love for little children. I hated to see them tormented with these demonic diseases. As I studied the Bible I read in John 10:10,

"The thief cometh not, but for to steal, and to kill, and to destroy: I am come that they might have life, and that they might have it more abundantly."

I realized the thief had tried to take that little boy's eyesight and make his life go very bad for him. From that point on, I was on a one-man mission to pray and lay hands on the sick, especially children. No matter what the cause. I started to see a mighty move of God in my life. Unlike the miracle with my daughter where there was little of my faith involved, with this one I saw the connection of my hands having power going out into this boy's eye. I realized that we play a major part because God uses our hands. (Mark 16:18) He uses us as a conduit of His power if we are a willing vessel. Although the Holy Spirit does the healing, unless a man or a woman steps out in faith and cooperates not much is going to happen.

I was being trained to do the work of an evangelist with signs and wonders. At the same time I was being blessed by the Lord to be a successful businessman.

Did I make some mistakes? More than I can count. It would be wrong to give the impression I followed the Spirit correctly 100% of the time. There were times I prayed for people when I wasn't really led by the Holy Spirit to do it. There were times that I didn't pray when I should have. There were times I got overzealous so the Lord had to show me the minefields so as not to step on the mines and blow myself up.

It may seem to some that my serving Christ on

the job was unusual. But the Bible teaches that this is normal Christianity. People are to see signs and wonders in their every day life. The Bible says in Mark 16:17 that "these signs shall follow them that believe" not just the full-time clergyman, but everyone who believes. If they follow you, that means they have to follow you on the job too. Jesus gave the great commission to all of us.

6

Under the Influence

Pastor Sam and Julie were associate pastors at the Assembly of God church where I grew up. The senior pastor had launched them to plant a church in the inner city and funded them for two or three years to get it started. Sharon and I felt led to go over and help work in this new church because we always had a love in our hearts for Black and Hispanic people. We worked there a number of years with Pastor Sam and Julie helping them build-up the work.

Pastor Sam was a little younger than I. He had graduated from an Assembly of God Bible school and always had a desire to start an inner city church. The Lord had called him specifically to work with the children there. He had a tremendous ability to relate to children and teens. They called the church

Outreach Assembly of God. They didn't have a building at first. They leased the basement of a tenement project. As the parents in the community saw he had a love for their children they gravitated to the church and then they eventually had to get a building. That's about the time Sharon and I joined the work.

It was a church that was geared toward youth at the beginning. Its members were made up of 80 % Black, 10% Hispanic and 10 % White. Everybody got along really well.

Eventually Pastor Sam put me on the leadership team as one of the deacons. Things were going smoothly. We had small but steady growth.

In 1993, I read in Charisma magazine that Rodney Howard-Brown was going to have a camp meeting in Louisville, Kentucky. I just started praying about it and felt the Lord was saying for me to contact Pastor Sam and ask him if he could take that week off and go at my expense.

I had seen a video clip on television from a Howard-Browne meeting at Oral Roberts University. Rodney and Kenneth Copeland were on the steps leading up to the platform and all of a sudden they started speaking in tongues to each other and both of them were like a couple of drunk people. That got my attention as I thought it was quite unusual. I wanted to see Rodney in person so I talked to Pastor Sam. He prayed about it and agreed to go. We went together and he dropped his wife and kids off at her parents on the way.

I really don't know what Pastor Sam hoped to see but I had a tremendous expectancy. We checked into a nearby hotel once we got there. The camp meeting was held in a huge convention center attended by six or seven thousand people. It was jam-packed.

I will never forget the first night we walked into the service. It lasted six hours. This was for a whole week. If you weren't into long services you were in the wrong place. Rodney came out the first night and began to minister. I can't tell you the subject. I really can't remember. I know he ministered a lot on the person and work of the Holy Spirit. All of a sudden in the section we are sitting in, this person and that person started falling on the floor laughing. They were falling out all over the place. There was a woman who was signing for the deaf and she got knocked right off her chair. There was nobody to sign for the deaf. She was sprawled out just rolling on the floor laughing. So I am enjoying this and having a good time. It was the first time I had seen anything like that.

This type of manifestation is clearly biblical. It can plainly be seen in the book of Acts. When the Holy Spirit was poured out on the day of Pentecost a crowd gathered to see what the commotion was. The Apostle Peter had to explain:

> *"But Peter, standing up with the eleven, lifted up his voice, and said unto them, Ye men of Judaea, and all ye that dwell at Jerusalem, be this known unto you, and hearken to my words:* **For these are not drunken, as ye suppose***, seeing it is but the third hour of the day. But this is that which was spoken by the prophet Joel; And it shall come to pass in the last days, saith God, I will pour out of my Spirit upon all flesh: and your sons and your daughters shall prophesy, and your young men shall see visions, and your old men shall dream dreams: And on my servants and on my handmaidens I will pour out in those days of my Spirit; and they shall prophesy…"*

(Acts 2:14-18 KJV)

When the Holy Spirit is poured out on people it can seem to the observer that they are drunk.

UNDER THE INFLUENCE

I looked over at Pastor Sam and I got the feeling he was not impressed to any degree. Sure enough, five hours later the service was over and we left. On our way out walking to the main doors he said, "Oh this is a bunch of nonsense! This stuff isn't real. If it was it would have hit you and I. We came down here seeking and being willing and if this was really a move of God then we would have got it."

So I'm just listening and not responding. I didn't want to get my enthusiasm diminished. I just said, "Maybe it will be better for you tomorrow."

So we left the building and we had to make a left hand turn to head towards the parking lot. The moment we turned, instantaneously we were both drunk as a skunk. We were bouncing off the convention building walls and we're saying to each other, "Did we drive here? Do we have a vehicle somewhere here? Where are we? What's going on here? Is this the parking lot? Did we park in a parking lot?"

We didn't know if we were on foot or horseback we were so drunk. Just moments before Sam said it was a bunch of nonsense and not the real deal. But we went from it being nonsense to like two drunken sailors on shore leave. We had all we could do to find my car and get back to the hotel. We collapsed in our beds like we had just closed the bar down at 3 a.m. We were gone. I have never touched a drop of alcohol in my life so I didn't even know what drunk felt like until this happened.

The next night we came back again. Pastor Sam was really excited. He realized he had misjudged this thing badly. The Lord has a sense of humor. When the Lord heard him say, "This is not the real deal" that was the moment that the Holy Spirit hit us. So now we both have a great expectancy for the service that night.

That night a who's who of Christian America was there. In attendance were 14 or 15 of the big pastors and evangelists of America. All were recognizable names. Brother Rodney invited them to come up on the platform and stand side by side where he could interview each of them. I think Richard Roberts was the first one he interviewed that night. Rodney said, "Richard, tell us what's going on at Oral Roberts University." His reply went something like this: "Well, Rodney, everything seems to be…" and then stammering and stumbling over his words he fell out under the power. Then the next one would come. "Tell me what's going on at your church." And the same thing would happen over and over again. The who's who of America were now flat out on their backs.

How Brother Rodney could even preach that night was beyond me. There was laughter that would just drown out the place, but he had the ability to block it out and just keep right on ministering. People were getting saved and people were filled with the Holy Spirit.

At the end of the second night, there was a little outdoor Italian restaurant that had stayed open because they knew they could get a lot of business from the crowd leaving that late. So Pastor Sam and I, both drunk as skunks again, walked over there and ordered a couple of meatball subs and some Cokes. The bill was about 16 or 17 dollars. We were so drunk in the Spirit that when we were done eating, we got up and left without paying the bill. The next morning I was in the shower and the Holy Spirit reminded me about the bill so I went back and paid it.

The Body of Christ has been hurt so badly and wounded from all directions. The Lord was using Rodney to get a "layer of hurt" off each night. It was like God was trying to get us freed up from lifetimes of abuse, bitterness, unforgiveness and anger. I think that is the purpose of holy laughter because the Bible says, "A merry heart doeth good like a medicine…" (Proverbs 17:22). It was like a healing process. That is how I would describe Rodney Howard-Browne's ministry.

After the meetings we were getting ready to drive back to Syracuse when Pastor Sam said, "Steve, instead of going home, my parents are only three and a half hours drive further south. We are carrying such a heavy anointing that we just received from the Holy Spirit. My family desperately needs what we've got. Would you mind if we took another day or two and go down there and see what the Lord might want to do?"

So we drove down there. On the way he called his father and told him we were coming. They called together all his cousins and aunts and uncles to meet us at the house. As we were driving all we talked about was what we had just experienced. We weren't laughing any more but the joy was still there. We were charged up.

We arrived at his parents' home and went in. There must have been at least 15 people, all his relatives. They had gathered in the living room. We didn't tell them anything that we had just experienced at Rodney's meetings. His mother had prepared a meal but we didn't eat it as I said to

Pastor Sam, "We have to minister to these people right now." All of a sudden he had a prophetic word for this one, and…boom…they went under the power. I had a word for the next one, and… boom…that one went under the power. They were drunk as skunks and we hardly even had time to get introduced to each other. The Holy Spirit used the power that we received at the conference with Rodney. All of his family members were sprawled out on the floor. I don't know what their religious background was but whatever it was they went from religion to Jesus real quick. There wasn't a person standing among them in just ten minutes time.

Now they are stumbling to their feet and laughing so hard they tried to escape us and get to other rooms. So we just followed them to other rooms and touched them again. When they got down into a kneeling position we just waved our hands at them and they went down again.

Sam's father seemed like a pretty reserved guy. He stumbled into this other room and I went in there and…boom…down he goes again. This is my pastor's father so I wanted to show the utmost respect to this man. But all of a sudden I felt myself kneeling down and I grabbed hold of his ankles and the lower part of his legs and I said, "The Lord says to tell you He is going to give you dancing feet again." At the same time I'm thinking, *What am I telling this guy? Have I lost my mind?* I kept saying to him, "The Lord imparts to you brother those dancing feet you once had, only this time you will dance in the Lord." Suddenly from his waist down his legs were flopping wildly all over the floor. I got aside and asked his wife, "Do you bear any witness to what I just said to him?" She said, "Brother Buza, in our younger days his passion in life was that he was a dancer. The only thing he enjoyed was dancing." I went back there to touch his legs again. Now he was not only laughing but those legs were just flying in every direction.

I'm thinking, "What in the world have we got ourselves in the middle of? People think Rodney is crazy and now they are going to think we are crazy right along with him."

We ministered nonstop from room to room. These people were trying to escape us because they couldn't physically take any more. You can only laugh so much before your sides start hurting, so they were trying to hide in different rooms and we were following them.

We ministered to them for 4 hours. It was close

to 10:00 at night when we stopped. They had expected us to come and have a meal and visit. Hours later the food was stone cold on the stove. I remembered spotting a Ponderosa on the way and I said to Pastor Sam, "I'm out of here! I'm taking my car. I've got to get a break from this. This is more than I can handle." So I drove back about a mile to where I had seen the Ponderosa. Fortunately, it was still open. I went in and got a steak dinner. I took my time because I was just physically spent. When I got back to the house an hour later I thought everybody was going to be calmed down. It was still going full bore. It went on like that for another hour and then it finally subsided.

Pastor Sam was so thrilled that the Holy Spirit honored his obedience to go and minister to his family. There were wounds from years and years ago that the Lord peeled away that evening.

We stayed overnight with them and then started on our drive back north. We picked Julie and the kids up and came back to Syracuse.

When I got home on Saturday I rested and didn't tell my wife too much about it. We went into our Sunday morning church service. As a deacon I always sat on the front row. I put my arm around my wife and when my arm went around her the power came on me again and she was slain in the spirit. She fell back in her chair and the service hadn't even started yet. I thought, "What in the world is going to happen here now?"

Pastor Sam started the worship service and it hit him. Now it's overflowing to the people. He never did preach. We had what happened in his parent's home happen all over again. The service went on for hours and hours. He had prepared a sermon but never got to give it.

For the next three years we moved in that anointing. There was such a glory cloud of God in the church. After a while I was trained to recognize it. I would know the second we walked into the foyer. I would say to Sharon, "Nobody is preaching here today," and sure enough nobody preached that day. Other times it wasn't quite so strong and I would say, "He will be able to preach today."

The church doubled in attendance. The Lord took people and birthed them into their gifting. It changed the inner city community near the church. To the best of my knowledge, we were the only church in the Syracuse area that was having a move of God.

We had a mighty move of the Holy Spirit but here's the sad part. I wish I could tell you that this move of God spread into our parent church in the suburbs but it didn't.

The last six months of the revival I kept saying to Pastor Sam, "Don't we owe this to our parent church to get in contact with the pastor there to let us come and do a Sunday night meeting to release this to their congregation?"

Then politics got into it and he said, "No brother, we may be misunderstood." I said, "Wait a minute here, this isn't "we," this is the Holy Spirit. What are you talking about "we" might be misunderstood? You don't have to apologize for what God is doing here. Don't you understand? He has entrusted you with the first revival to ever hit Syracuse. Even Charles Finney couldn't get something going here. This has been dumped right in your lap and you don't want to share it? We've got to take this and release it to the main church."

He knew I was telling him the Word of the Lord, but Pastor Sam didn't want to experience the reproach and misunderstanding that Rodney Howard-Browne endured. So he attempted a "minor version" and invited a select group from the main church to a Saturday night service at the inner city church.

The night of the meeting Pastor Sam did not

share or preach about our experiences. It was sanitized to where we had a nice little service and nothing much happened.

At the end of the service I said to myself: *I'm a leader here and this man doesn't want to let the Holy Spirit flow. I'm going to go up there and make myself available.* I didn't even say a word. I just stood up there. Then a few people came up and they were slain in the spirit. It broke out to a minor degree but overall the meeting grieved the Spirit and soon after that the revival came to an end.

In defense of Pastor Sam, there are not many who will risk jobs and the support of their families for the controversial. **There is a price to be paid if you want a move of God.** If your children were young and you depended upon a church denomination for your living, would you put everything at risk?

7

Back From the Dead

It was like the Lord dropped a mantle on me and said: "You can move into this area now. Do not be worried because I have given you power over the devil." That was my experience in the case of Danny. It was like the Lord gave me a special grace for it.

Obviously God is the healer but it doesn't appear to be a hard thing when you get that anointing to rest on you.

At the time we had recently become members of a new church. When we had an interview with Pastor Lee before we joined, he asked about our spiritual gifts. I could tell he was excited to have us there. He was the kind of pastor that encouraged members to develop and use the gifts of the Holy Spirit. I told Pastor Lee that Sharon and I were in ministry at a previous church and we went through some battles. I asked him to let us rest for a year or so. I said: "This is what I would like you to do. I am not going to come to you and tell you when it is time to utilize us in the church. I believe the Lord will tell you when we have rested enough. When He does, then you come and tell me in what capacity you would like us to minister to the Body of Christ."

We weren't in a big hurry to be used in ministry. But on a Wednesday night one of the Church elders named Bud came up to the front of the church. We knew Bud and his wife Wanda very well. He was pretty down in the dumps and by the way he started out I knew whatever he was going to say wasn't going to be very good:

"Folks, Pastor Lee just gave me the mike for a few minutes before we close the service. One of my employees named Danny has had five strokes back to back and the doctors have been begging his wife and kids to pull the plug. He has been lying there in a brain dead coma in the hospital in Syracuse for seven days."

Bud was not asking prayer for Danny. Bud considered him already a dead man because the doctors told him he was brain dead and even if he lived he would be a vegetable. He was asking the church to pray for the family, that the wife would get the courage to pull the plug and the children would get a peace to be able to do that.

As he was finishing up a really strong unction of the Holy Spirit came on me and I heard the voice of the Lord in my spirit say, "He's not to die. I want you to go and raise him from the dead tomorrow morning." I heard it so clear. I also heard, "I want you to take Pastor Lee with you. I want him to see this. Wait till the service is over and let everybody file out so you don't draw attention to yourself. When the church is empty tell Pastor Lee what I just told you."

I called Pastor Lee over. Remember that I had already told him that I didn't want to be used in any kind of ministry. About a year had already gone by since I had told him that I would let him tell me when I was ready. But three weeks prior he thought I had a prophetic word in a service. He said: "Steve if you have a word bring it forth. I'm ready to release you now." Because he had already done that earlier I wasn't afraid to approach him with this.

You have to bear in mind I wasn't on his leadership team at this time. I was to be on his leadership team six months later, but I had no position in the church at this time. I told him, "I have to make myself a little vulnerable with you. I think so far you believe I am a fairly credible member of your congregation. I don't know if what I am about to tell you will be hard for you to deal with or not, but I have to deliver this message. As Bud was asking for prayer for the family to be okay during this time of grief that is coming up with the funeral, I heard the Holy Spirit tell me, 'He's not to die. I want you to go and raise him from the dead tomorrow morning.' He wants to raise Danny back from the dead. Here's the part I'm hesitant to ask you. He told me to have you go with me."

My heart was probably beating almost 200 beats per minute. I guess this was because the first time I told him I wanted to do ministry was that I felt led to raise someone from the dead! But the Holy Spirit had already prepared Pastor Lee for this. He said: "Steve, thank you for making yourself vulnerable to tell me that. All day long today at the office I kept hearing the Lord say, "I want to raise him from the dead. Are you willing?" I dismissed it because I don't move in that type of a gift. I have never moved in that area. To be honest with you, I was afraid to take this on for fear that nothing would not happen. As Bud and Wanda's pastor I would be more than glad to accompany you tomorrow morning."

As we drove to the hospital in the morning I asked him if he wanted to be the one to minister to Danny. He said, "No brother. I told you last night I don't work in this gift. I'm assuming you do or the Lord wouldn't have talked to you and told you to come and pray for him. I'm going to pass on this and watch you."

So we got there. Neither one of us had ever met Danny's wife. She was sitting there by herself. The children were not there. I knelt down and took her hand and told her who I was and introduced Pastor Lee to her. I said, "Would you mind if I lay my hand on him and pray for him? The Lord wants to bring your husband back from the dead. He is not going to die." She asked, "How do you know that?" I said, "I can't explain it to you in a way that would make sense to you but I "know that I know" the Lord spoke to me in our Wednesday night church service that He wants to bring him back to life." She said, "Steve, he has had five strokes, he is brain dead. He can't come back to life. For the last four days every doctor on this floor has been begging me to pull the plug. My children are furious at me. They want me to do it too."

The Lord just gave me wisdom. I said to her, "How long has he been laying there?"

She said, "Seven days."

"You loved him enough to stay in that chair for seven days, right?"

And I heard from the Lord, "Ask her if she loves him enough to give me four more days to heal him."

I told her, "The Spirit of God just spoke to my spirit and said to ask you: 'Do you love him enough to give four more days with today being day one?' The Lord says to tell you to give him four more days and you will have your husband back. You have sat here for seven days, is he worth four more days?" She said, "It is worth however long it takes."

I said, "Let me do the believing and you just trust me that I am a man of God and I have heard from the Lord and put it all on me. I will take all the responsibility for the believing for it. If four days from now you pull the plug and he dies, I will face you like a man and say I missed it. Can we leave it at that and have that kind of arrangement?"

All of a sudden, hope started to come into her

and she said, "You really believe this, don't you?"

I said, "Without a shadow of a doubt I do. Can I pray for him now? The Holy Spirit is a gentleman. I won't even attempt to believe God for a miracle unless you tell me you are in agreement with this."

She said, "I've got nothing to lose, do I?" She said to go ahead and pray for him.

Pastor Lee got on one side of him and I got on the left hand side of him next to the wife and I laid my hands on him. I started talking to Danny because I believe people who are brain dead can hear everything that is going on because the spirit is very much alive. I talked to the spirit part of him, not the flesh.

I said, "Danny, this is Pastor Lee standing to the one side of you and I am Steve Buza, a member of his congregation. Jesus is going to give you a second chance at life. I am going to lay my hands on you right now and the Holy Spirit is going to come on you and your body and your brain are going to start to be healed from this very minute. We have got permission from your wife so get ready to receive the healing power of God right now."

Then I prayed: "Holy Spirit I release your power to go into Danny now to affect the healing. I

command all damaged brain cells to be totally dis-
solved out of his body and you will replace every
single brain cell that was damaged. I command total
restoration of this man from head to toe in Jesus'
name. No effects of the stroke will remain four
days from now and he will arise from this brain-
dead coma totally well with no aftereffects whatsoever. He will be every bit whole within four days. I
thank you for hearing this prayer and I release your
power now to do its work in Jesus name."

I told him, "Danny. Pastor Lee and I will see
you in four days. We will be back."

I then turned away from him and I went back
to Danny's wife and said: "We will see you four
days from now."

She said, "Oh, I hope you are right."

She squeezed my hand like a desperate woman
would squeeze a hand. I could see more faith in
her eyes than when we first got there.

That was day one. Nothing happened the rest
of that day. Nothing happened the second day.
Nothing happened the third day. Two-thirty in the
afternoon of day four, he sat right up out of a
brain-dead coma and started pulling the tubes out
of his arms and body.

He said, "Where are we? Get me some food

honey, I'm starving." The nurses came and said, "You can't pull these tubes out." He said, "I've got to get them out, they are irritating me. Besides, I told my wife to get me some food. What am I doing here anyhow?"

I found out about an hour after it happened. We had left a phone number and Danny's wife called Pastor Lee. I was coming home from a job to get something at my office around 3:30 and I wasn't there for more than 15 minutes when the phone rang. It was Pastor Lee's wife, Averell.

My wife Sharon was all excited and she told me: "Averell's on the phone. She says that Pastor Lee wants to talk to you."

"I know what he wants to talk to me about. He's going to tell me we need to go see Danny."

"How do you know that? He hasn't even told you what he wants."

"You'll see. I know."

I got on the phone. "Pastor what can I do for you?"

He said, "Steve. He woke up! He woke up! He woke up!"

"I know that. I knew it four days ago."

About an hour later, we arrived at the hospital. The family was ecstatic. The wife was ecstatic.

It shocked the doctors. It shook them to the core of their being. They had no way of explaining it. They had to admit it was a miracle. Twenty-eight days later Danny was back to work. No sign of any illness whatsoever. Not a single thing wrong with his body. The doctors spent most of the 28 days checking him out to verify that he was a medical miracle or he would have been back to work sooner. They ran every test on him looking for damage. They tried to figure it out, but they couldn't find a thing wrong.

The Boy Who Hung Himself

It was in 1995 when my mother phoned and told me that my Aunt Kate's 15-year-old grandson had hung himself. He hung himself in the basement. His siblings came downstairs to find him there. They called 911 and the ambulance came and picked him up.

I had gone to get something from my office at home and as I walked in the door Sharon said, "I think you will have to drop what you are doing, Steve, and go to Community Hospital." Someone had called Sharon and told her about the boy and what hospital he was in.

I didn't know this particular boy, but Sharon felt that I should go to the hospital and pray for him, as they did not expect him to live.

As soon as Sharon told me to go, I had a strong witness that this was another one of those divine appointments. As I was walking out the door the Lord said, "Go back and use your phone and call your daughter Sarah. I want her to see what it going to happen in this situation." So I called her and sure enough, she was home.

I asked, "Can you get away?"

She said, "Yes, why?"

"I will explain to you on the way. I'm coming in to get you in a few minutes"

When we got to the hospital, the family wasn't in the room but we were still allowed to go in. He was totally brain-dead. They had him on life support system. We were told that even if he lived he would be a vegetable.

I asked my daughter Sarah to go on one side of the bed and I would go on the other side.

I talked to him and said, "I have never met you before but I am Steve Buza and this is my daughter Sarah. Young man, you are very fortunate because the Lord had mercy on you. He sent me here to

pray for you. He is going to bring you back to life."
And I said, "I have heard about the lifestyle you
have been living. Don't go back and do the things
you have been doing before, because the second
time you may not get another chance. Now I am
going to pray for you."

Then I prayed and said something like, "Holy
Spirit I come to you in Jesus name and I just ask
you right now to touch this young man from the
top of his head to the bottom of his toes. I command any affects of this hanging to be null and
void and wiped away by the blood of Jesus. I command all new brain cells to come into his brain. Let
there be no permanent damage whatsoever. I ask
that you wake him up quickly out of this coma and
that he will walk out of this hospital with a new
lease on life. I thank you that you hear and answer
prayer. I thank you Holy Spirit that you are the
healer and not us. Sarah and I just thank you for
this miracle in Jesus Name."

When I got done praying I looked over at Sarah
and she said, "Dad why did you bring me here?
He's no different. Why didn't he sit up?

I said, "Sarah, these things don't always happen instantly. The Bible says to lay hands on the
sick and they will recover. If he sprang right up,

that would be a miracle. But most healings are not miracles. Most of them are recoveries. Obviously this is going to be a recovery type of healing, but you are going to see it."

We left the hospital around noon and I took Sarah back home. About 4:30 that afternoon my aunt called my home. Sharon reached me on the job and she told me: "It happened again. He's out of a brain-dead coma. He's totally well and they're going to release him soon." A day or two after that phone call, they let him leave the hospital.

My aunt had been backslidden at the time. She had started drinking heavily because of a bad marriage. My uncle had driven her into a state of depression. I think having witnessed that miracle with her grandson brought her back to the Lord.

Four or five years later Sharon and I got word that she was dying. We went to visit and she was awake but she couldn't talk. She had lost her communicative skills. I took her hand and she looked up at me and smiled the best she could.

I said, Aunt Kate, I am here just for one reason and you know what it is. I know you slipped away from the Lord. Have you made things right between you and Jesus?"

She just blinked a couple of times with her eyes.

(I said, "Blink twice if you are okay with Jesus.")
She got a little bigger smile.

I said, "So, I don't have to pray with you again to get saved?" She blinked once indicating no and she smiled. She made it to heaven by the skin of her teeth, but praise God she made it. I know she is now with my dad in heaven.

Again, it wasn't me. It was the power of the Holy Spirit of God that not only saved a young man's life, but a grandmother's soul as well.

8

Our First Trip to India

Sharon and I had been members at Faith Chapel for 14 months when Pastor Lee called me into his office. He said, Steve. Sit down. I need to talk to you. He continued, "I've got this offer that came to me just a short time ago from a Reverend Thomas in the southern tip of India. I really prayed about this before I called you. I have checked this with the Holy Spirit and I felt led to offer you a chance to take my place to minister there for 18 days of meetings as an evangelist."

I was somewhat surprised. Pastor Lee had an eldership team of four or five very capable elders. I knew who they were because Sharon and I had become friends with all of them. I asked him why he didn't send one of them.

He said, "I know that you can preach and this

requires a preacher, not a teacher. These will be revival meetings and that is your gift."

"How do you know you can trust me with that?"

"I thought this out and prayed this out very carefully before I asked you here today. I am not asking for an immediate answer but I would appreciate it if you would talk with your wife and pray about it and get back to me when you can."

Sharon and I talked and prayed about it. About a week later I went back to him and said we would be willing to do it under one condition. I wanted to talk with Reverend Thomas myself so I could get a feel for the flavor of ministry he wanted us to do. Pastor Lee said that was fine and gave me the contact information. So I phoned Rev. Thomas and began to see that the Lord was really in this thing.

When I talked to him he seemed very excited about having us take Pastor Lee's place. It didn't seem to be a problem for him. It turned out that he was coming to the US in a few weeks and landing in JFK. So I offered to meet him and have dinner with him. Three weeks later Sharon and I took a day off and got to JFK a couple of hours ahead of his plane coming in. We had a wonderful and cordial dinner. He shared with us that he was the overseer of 50 churches. He wanted an evangelist to come and preach to the lost. We felt that it was the Lord and accepted.

This open door to India was not totally unexpected. For many years the Lord had been preparing me for this event. Several times I had been "picked out" by men and women of God in church services around the country. The prophetic words all went something like this: "Sir, before long God is going to expand your ministry. He has been working with you and developing your gifts. Very shortly your gifts are going to go out to the world as well as this country. He is going to use you in a mighty way. He is going to have you minister to multitudes of people all over this world to a degree that you can't comprehend. Get ready. The Lord has his hand on your life and he is going to use you in a spectacular way."

Sharon and I were excited to get our passports and visas to India. Finally the day came for our long flights. We traveled the better part of two days. We flew from Syracuse to Detroit; Detroit to Amsterdam; Amsterdam to Mumbai; Mumbai to Chennai and then the last flight to Trivandrum. It was a very long trip with long layovers.

Pastor Thomas met us and we stayed at his

Bible school during the meetings. This trip was where we really started to feel the working of miracles and the gift of faith as the Bible describes them. We started to feel those accelerate and operate in our lives.

The crusade meetings were at night, so we would teach during the morning in the Bible school. One morning we had 55 pastors and their wives attending. All of a sudden the back door to the classroom flew open and we heard a little boy let out a howl. They brought in one of the pastor's sons. He was a little boy about five or six years old. He had taken a horrible fall onto the concrete sidewalk one floor below. I had played a lot of sports so I recognized a serious knee injury when I saw it. A couple of men brought him in and they gave him to his father. All of a sudden, I knew in my spirit what to do. I told Pastor Thomas to have them bring the boy to me. I just knew instinctively that the Lord wanted to do a miracle to demonstrate his power to the people. I had Pastor Thomas take a seat next to me and I held the little boy in my lap. In the United States he would have had major surgery on his knee and would be in physical therapy for the next several months. As I laid my hand on his knee I prayed, "Holy Spirit of God, I ask you to have compassion on this little boy right now and touch his knee and just heal it."

As soon as I got those words out of my mouth I felt two invisible hands like a surgeon's working right underneath the kneecap. I said to Sharon, "Honey, come here. You've got to see this!"

She said, "What in the world is this!"

I said, "That's the Holy Spirit operating on his knee."

You could literally feel invisible hands doing stuff on his knee. That lasted for about four or five minutes or so. Rev. Thomas was pretty amazed as he was holding his legs across his knees. Just as fast as it started, it stopped. The Holy Spirit said, "He is healed. Put him down and have him start walking now."

Through the interpreter I said to tell the little boy that he is okay and to start walking. He started walking up and down. He ran back and forth. Everyone was in tears. The Holy Spirit had created a new knee for this little boy and the parents were happy. They released the boy and he ran out to continue playing and we continued on with the pastors' conference.

One of the pastors' wives who saw the miracle of the little boy contacted a friend who lived about two hours away to invite her to come to the evening service. She was dying of cancer. The woman said it would be very hard for her to travel two hours in her condition over rough roads and then sit in a service for another two or three hours. She said, "If you can get the evangelist to come off the platform near the entrance so he can pray for me and then take me immediately home, I will agree to come." She explained she was desperate and dying but just didn't have the physical strength to sit through a service with a lot of music and preaching that goes with a Healing Festival. So the woman that invited her said she would come transport her to the meeting and get me to pray for her. I didn't know any of this.

That night I was going into the service when I recognized this young gal from the Bible school. She grabbed me and said, "You have to pray for my friend here. She said she is dying of cancer. She just came here to be prayed for and she wants to immediately go home. She doesn't want to insult you but she is not physically fit to stay."

Sharon was standing next to me. As I looked at the woman with cancer I could see the yellow color of death on her. Even worse, her body had filled with fluid so her arms and her legs were oversized.

As I touched her arm it was like pressing on a water balloon. I said, "Sharon and I will just cast this thing off of her right now. This does not require a healing. This is a demonic attack on her body. That's all this is."

I said to Sharon, "Honey put your hand on her arm." I put my hand on her other arm and said, "You foul spirit of cancer... I break your power over this woman right now. I command you to be gone and leave this body right now." As soon as I said that all the fluid in her body just went down. We watched it immediately disappear right out of her body. We could feel muscle again. Her color changed and she was set free of that demonic thing instantly. The whole thing didn't take a minute. Her friend said, "Okay we can leave now. I can take you home." The woman said, "Oh no. I feel like I'm young again. Anybody that can have that kind of power that their God supplies them, I want to hear what he has to say."

They went and sat in the second or third row from the front. She insisted on staying for the whole service. She was a Hindu lady. She gave her heart to the Lord on the spot and she stayed for the entire night and enjoyed it immensely.

There was a young associate pastor from a big

church in Maryland attending the meetings. Pastor Thomas wanted me to let him do some preaching because he had flown in unexpectedly. Pastor Thomas asked if I would mind sharing the service for a couple of nights. I said sure, and so the young pastor went first and then I finished the service for two or three nights.

One of the nights before the service, Sharon overheard a conversation between two elderly high-ranking officials in the denomination.

She heard them talking about how the young man had the knowledge but the older man had the anointing. They came back to the Bible school in the morning with credentials and paperwork all filled out and ordained me into their denomination. It was the Pentecostal Church of God. I found out when I got back into the United States that their denomination has over two thousand churches in America and that they also accepted my ordination here.

Before my ordination the young pastor would sit with me for hours back at the Bible school. We would sit in some lawn chairs and he kept asking, "Are you sure you are not ordained?" Are you sure you didn't go to Bible school?"

He was taught that you had to go to Bible

College in order to have a ministry. He would look at me like I was some different kind of species. He was astonished that I could minister without having some kind of a sheepskin in my hand. I kept telling him, "No. I haven't had a formal training. As a matter of fact, I'm still a layman at the church where I attend. I'm not even an Elder of the church."

I realized that it's better to have the anointing than to just have the knowledge. My training came from walking with Jesus for over 40 years. Jesus had me in His "Bible School of Life." There is a place for systematic Bible study and knowledge, but it can never substitute for the School of the Holy Spirit. That is where you get your anointing. That is where you get the "gold tried in the fire."

As we were flying out of India from Mumbai to Amsterdam we looked down at the landscape. I said to Sharon, "I will never be the same, Honey. I left half of my heart back there with those people. I'm going home with half a heart and I just pray that some day we get a chance to come back here and do this again because these are wonderful, wonderful people. These Indian people are such precious people to the Lord." We just wept and wept.

9

The Amsterdam Connection

On our way back to the United States something happened at the airport in Amsterdam that was to forever change our life. I call it the "Amsterdam Connection."

After the domestic flights in India, we finally had gotten on the plane heading to Amsterdam. By that time we were pretty exhausted. It was about 6:10 in the morning and just barely light out when we landed. We were going to have a seven and a half hour layover before our next flight left for the United States. Little did I realize it was going lead to one of the final pieces of my development as an evangelist.

After two hours of sitting with Sharon and reading some materials, I remembered seeing a sign saying they had a McDonald's in the airport. In India, you can't get a hamburger because the cows are considered sacred. I was craving some beef, so I asked Sharon if she wanted to go with me and get a burger and a coke or something. She told me "No, I think I will just read my book and stay here."

After walking to the McDonald's I saw a big line had formed. I thought how in the world can all these people want a hamburger this early in the morning? I didn't want to wait in that long line and I had to use the restroom. I saw a restroom sign about a hundred feet down the hall. I walked in and there's a guy about 6'4" and 275 pounds. He was nothing but just solid muscle. As I saw him leaning against the wall I was just happy to see another American.

Normally, I am not like this in public, but I walked over to him and said, "Hi. I'm Steve Buza. What's your name?"

He said, "I'm Jim Gysbers, nice to meet you."

We asked each other where we were from. I found out he was from Wisconsin. He told me he had been ministering in India for the last six weeks with an evangelist named Mark Swiger. They traveled all over India doing massive Gospel Festivals with tens of thousands of people. I told Jim I was down in Trivandrum doing meetings for 18 days.

They had just gotten off the same flight we did, coming from Mumbai. The reason Jim was leaning on the restroom wall was that he was waiting for one of the stalls to be open. The next thing that happened just amazes me to this day. The door opened on one of those stalls and Jim said, "Don't leave this restroom! I HAVE to introduce you to Brother Mark. Stay right here!"

Now if you value your life and a guy 6'-4" and 275 pounds with nothing but chiseled granite muscle tells you to stay in the bathroom you are not moving. I didn't know it then, but it was a God connection. This guy was just so interesting I figured what have I got to lose? I will meet whomever he wants me to meet. I was going to have a hamburger so I'll have it with him and this evangelist Mark Swiger.

I told him not to worry as I had to use one of the stalls too. As we finished and washed our hands Jim said, "You are really going to love this guy." I said, "I'll tell you what I am going to love more than meeting Mark. If that line is clear I am going to love meeting with a quarter pounder with cheese, fries and a diet coke, then I will go with you to meet whomever you want me to meet."

He just laughed and went with me to get my food. I came around the corner with my tray to find a seat and there was Mark Swiger. Mark was tall and looked to be about 10 years younger than myself. We spent about an hour and or so together. We compared notes and talked shop a little about what we had been doing in India. Even though nothing usually ever comes of it, we exchanged addresses and phone numbers. We said goodbye and I thought it was nice to meet some fellow ministers. Then I went back to catch up with Sharon.

Sometimes when God is doing something you don't realize it. About eight weeks later I got a phone call one night and the voice on the other end of the line said, "Hi, Steve. This is Mark Swiger."

"Excuse me. I don't recognize your voice," I replied.

"I'm Mark Swiger. We met at the airport in Amsterdam."

"Oh forgive me. I only talked to you that one time."

We had a nice talk for a few minutes and then he cut right to what he had called about.

"Steve, every time I have tried to pray for the last three or four days, it's like I see your face in front of me. I hear the Lord saying to call you and invite you and your wife to come visit our home in Hollis, Maine. You have got to come and meet with me and my wife."

I told him I would talk to my wife about it and would get back to him. Several days went by before I called him back with an answer. Sharon and I felt that maybe something was happening here that could be a divine connection. We didn't want to miss anything if this was of God. We also saw no harm in people of God spending three or four days together. We went to see where this would take us, never knowing it would take us around the world again and again.

We set up a time a week or two after the holidays and drove from Syracuse up to their home in Maine. An incredible thing happened the minute we arrived. We unloaded our suitcases and came up the stairs onto the porch and into the living room. We looked out the window and all of a sudden a freezing rain began to fall. Within an hour all of the tires on Mark's car and all of the tires on our van were encased in ice. We were literally stuck there for the next 3 days. I'm not the smartest guy in the world, but when I saw both of our vehicles stuck in the ice I thought, "Something is going on here." There would be no sightseeing or going out to eat, just the four of us in prayer and fellowship.

Mark and I had already met in Amsterdam but Sharon was a little apprehensive about meeting Mark and his wife Paulette for the first time. She soon found out she didn't have anything to be nervous about. Paulette and Sharon had a lot of things in common and clicked right away. We were all able to talk like people who knew each other for a long time.

Mark soon got around to explaining why he felt led to invite us. He had been a pastor for 20 years before God called him to evangelize India. He had learned many things about evangelism and working in India—many the "hard way." He explained the Lord had put on his heart to help mentor us. He felt in his spirit to impart his years of experience, not just what he had learned in India, but from being in ministry for over 20 years.

Our first trip to India had been fruitful, but it also exposed many areas that we knew little or nothing about. Not just culturally, but the "how's and why's" of evangelism. We were still babies at ministry. Mark saw God's desire to use me in evangelism and impact multitudes, but for that to happen it would require more training and mentoring in some areas.

Those three days at the Swiger's home seemed to fly by. We left knowing that my next trip to India would be to travel with Mark and assist him.

My first trip to India with Mark Swiger lasted seven weeks. In those seven weeks I learned more about ministry than I had before in my entire life.

It was a walking Bible school—a school of the Spirit. We traveled from city to city doing mass meetings. Between his preaching and ministry, I was constantly asking Mark questions and getting answers. Why did you do it that way? Why did you say that? Why did you handle that situation that way? Why did you preach that way?

I could never have learned in years of Bible school what I learned in seven weeks traveling with Mark on the firing lines. Mark said he was doing for me what he wished somebody had done for him. It was really training of a higher order. It must have been how Jesus trained the disciples.

In the past, other ministers had looked down on me because I had no "formal training." Had I gone off to Bible school somewhere I couldn't have learned what I needed. I would have walked away with a piece of paper, but teachers do not know the secrets and insights of an evangelist. So I did get "formal training" after all, and it was the best I could ever get.

Sharon and I often said afterwards we felt the main reason we went to India the first time was to meet Mark and Paulette. Jim Gysbers, the man I met in the Amsterdam restroom, told me the main reason God sent him to India that trip was to have him introduce me to Mark.

In the months before we left for India, God blessed my business. I was able to line up enough remodeling and construction work to keep my crews busy all the time I was gone and longer.

I learned so many things that trip. My faith increased tremendously from listening to Mark preach and seeing all the thousands of salvations and miraculous healings. I learned there was much more to ministry than I thought. The preaching part is 5 % and the preparation is 95 %.

People just don't know what goes on behind the scenes. Being naïve and just being in India once before I thought, "Mark's just going to show up, he's going to walk up on the platform and minister for four nights, thousands of things are going to happen and it's going to be wonderful." Although those things did happen, they came with a cost—always with a cost. Little did I know until I traveled with him for seven weeks that it was very, very hard work.

We traveled on rough, dangerous roads at all hours of the day and night. We didn't have decent quarters to sleep in, a place to bathe, or even the use of a toilet. We were being pursued by political extremists who were trying to kill us.

I saw several times how the Lord gave Mark the knowledge to be one step ahead and how it saved our lives. It was like an Indiana Jones movie where the enemy was always one step behind us. Fortunately, Mark was given divine strategies so they couldn't harm us--although they came very close a number of times!

I realized the preaching was almost the easiest part because that's a gift from the Holy Spirit. It was the work behind the scenes that nobody sees that is also important. Like when people make a movie in Hollywood. You see the cast and the directors, the assistant directors, the cinematographers, the lighting people, and the costume people. At the end the movie credits roll listing hundreds of people. You see John Wayne was the star, but really without these other people behind the scenes, John Wayne could not have been the star.

EXPLOITS IN THE MIRACULOUS

Some of the things I learned about: How to work with the police and existing political system; how some things you could do in some locations you couldn't do in others; working with interpreters, both good and bad; staff relations; people have their own agenda; everybody wasn't as committed to the kingdom of God as we were; working in an environment of graft and corruption; diplomacy; advertising; promotion and publicity; video and photography; television and radio broadcasting; printing; working with members of the press; working with churches and pastors; local customs; the physical arrangements of the grounds; lighting; sound system; electrical power generation; seating; platforms; musicians and choirs; prayer teams; ushers; volunteer training; crowd control; offerings and accounting; forming and working with various committees; government permits; vendors; public transportation; follow-up; etc. etc.

It was quite an experience just to see Mark navigate through these mine fields to eventually end up on the platform to present the gospel to the people.

I wasn't just observing Mark. He put me to work that first trip. In every town church leaders and government officials wanted to meet and spend time with Mark. If we let everybody do that he wouldn't have had a moment of peace. He liked to shut himself in his room before the meetings praying and spending time with the Lord. I was able to make that possible by meeting with people in his place. Also Mark could not go into the crowds to lay hands on the sick during the meetings because the crowds would react and people would crush each other. He would pray a "mass prayer" and the Lord would move through the crowd healing the people. But many would come in the afternoons or stay late after the night services hoping for a personal touch. I was able to do that without causing crowd control problems. Because of that I saw the Lord do some wonderful miracles through my hands.

I saw many, but one I will cherish for the rest of my life.

A young Hindu boy about 10 years old came in the afternoon prayer line. His left arm was wrapped in a dirty white rag that was tied around his neck. My interpreter asked the father to tell me his story before I prayed. He said they came from a distant village. He heard about the meetings and he brought his son from a long way away. His son had an accident and cracked his elbow about three and a half months ago. It shattered. He was just a poor farmer and couldn't afford any medical treatment. The father did the only thing he could do. He set the bones back in place as well as he could and wrapped the arm with a bicycle chain. Then he took a white rag and made a sling for him. His arm has been in that position for three and a half months. The father said if they didn't get a miracle from God it was very likely his arm was going to be frozen in that position for the rest of his son's life.

With that information I laid my hand on the sling where his elbow was and commanded the power of God to come into that arm and do a miracle. I spoke that the elbow would be healed instantly in the name of Jesus and there would be no aftereffects or any problem with that elbow ever again.

As I just lightly touched it, the boy shrieked in pain. He took his other arm and pushed me away saying, No...No...No! I looked at the father and I told him to tell his son to obey what I am telling him to do. Then, very carefully under the leading of the Holy Spirit, I started to unwind the white rag and exposed the arm. It was all mangled and by this time this kid was almost passing out with pain. He begged me to stop. I told him through the interpreter, "No, I'm not stopping. Just trust me. I know what I'm doing."

When I finally took the last piece of cloth off and took the bicycle chain off I said to my interpreter, "Let's you and I stand about ten feet away from him lest the people think you and I are the healers." We moved back. Immediately the Holy Spirit started at the wrist, took his arm and straightened it out more and more and more. Then it just locked right in place. Everybody there let out a gasp because they had seen the wound on the boy's elbow. Now there wasn't any wound. He had a 100% miraculous healing. I had the boy move his arm up behind his head and twist it everyway possible. There was no doubt we had seen a wonderful miracle.

That night Mark had the father and the boy come up during the evening meeting and give their testimony.

I've always had a heart to see people healed, especially young children. It just tears me up to see young children deformed or maimed or anything like that. That set the stage for something major that happened in one of the Gospel Festivals.

Mark had cautioned me many times to be

careful how we pray for the sick in the city-wide meetings. He explained that people always want to come up for healing prayer while you are preaching. If you do, it disrupts and the crowd will get out of control. So, for the sake of getting one person healed, it could cost thousands of people their eternal souls. That was why we prayed for the sick in a mass prayer at the end of the service or laid hands on them after most of the people had left the grounds. Mark told me so many times it should have been ingrained in my spirit to never do such a thing. But one night as Mark was preaching I saw a group of women in the crowd near the left side of the platform where I was seated.

They held up this little boy who was probably seven or eight years old. I assumed it was the mother and some of her friends. Mark was preaching and they couldn't get his attention. They knew that I was his co-evangelist, traveling with him. So they got my attention and held the little boy up towards me. I could see that from his waist up he was totally normal but from his waist down his legs were like spaghetti. They were impossibly thin and hung like rags. They appeared boneless. It was obvious he had never walked.

Mark was just getting ready to give the altar

call for people to get saved. My heart went out to the boy so much that, even though I knew that I was disobeying Mark's instructions, I motioned for the mother to bring the child to the side of the platform.

I slipped over very quietly to the side because I knew if Mark saw me I was in big trouble. They handed him up to me and I took him as far towards the back of the platform as I possibly could. I wasn't thinking that what I was about to do would shift the crowd's attention from Mark giving the altar call to me holding this boy up into the night sky.

I held this boy up with all the fervor that I could muster in my spirit and prayed, "Holy Spirit of God, if you ever answered a prayer that I've ever asked in my life, give this little boy a miracle and develop two brand new legs right now." The second I cried that out to the Lord electricity shot right down through my body. I could feel it go right down my arms and right into the boy's body. Instantaneously he had two brand new legs.

I wanted to enjoy the moment with the boy, his mother and the other women, so I had him walk back and forth on the platform. I was going all the way to the end and all the way back. Mark was in the middle of the altar call so I thought, "That's okay, Mark's doing his thing and I'm doing mine." That's how I rationalized it. I made sure I was just looking down at the floor. I didn't even want to make eye contact with Mark because I knew if I did, I was in a world of trouble. Because of my inexperience I thought that the mother, the little boy and the group of women with her were the only ones watching. But they weren't the only ones watching. As I was walking back and forth with the boy I heard a major commotion. I thought I had better look over in Mark's direction. I turned and saw the crowd mobbing the platform. They had broken through all the barricades and here they came, the whole 15 thousand of them. All of a sudden I couldn't even see the platform. People were falling and the platform was littered with people from one end to the other.

The most fearful moment of all my adventures with Mark in India was about to take place. He turned and looked at me. Even though he didn't talk, his eyes said, "What did you do?" All of a sudden he started wading through the mass of people. He took the child from me and handed him to one of the pastors and told him to give him back to his mother. Then he grabbed my arm and I thought he would pull my arm right out of its socket. Above the pandemonium he yelled, "Come on with me. We've got to get out of here!" Riot had broken out. They were mobbing the platform and it could collapse any second. To save my life and the lives of people that would have been trampled Mark pulled me with him.

We pushed our way down the ramp on the right hand side of the platform where our vehicle was waiting. The driver was already inside and we got in the vehicle just quick enough to lock the doors. I thought they were going to tip it over because all of a sudden you couldn't see out the windows. There were just so many people wanting to break into that car to get us to come out and pray for the sick. The car was completely surrounded by a sea of people. Mark told the driver: "Start very slowly at first. Do not stop blowing the horn. Slowly, keep the car moving." It took a long time, but we eventually inched through the crowd and it thinned to where we could finally break free.

I knew what was coming next. Mark is always a man of God. He never spoke to me without wisdom. He took a few minutes to gain his composure and said, "Didn't I tell you never to do that in a city-wide meeting? Do you see what happens when you don't do things in order? I'm compassionate like you. I operate in that gift too. He could have been healed later during the mass prayer or you could have prayed for him after the service. What would his healing mean if the hospital was filled with broken bones and dead bodies?"

I made more trips to India with Mark over the next several years. Each time I learned more and gained more experience. Eventually Mark set it up so that I did my own Gospel Festival.

While often the meetings were dangerous and the lessons I learned difficult, our travels were not without humor. We also had some laughs and good times.

When we were leaving a Gospel Festival one night and getting ready to go back to the hostel where we were staying, unbeknownst to us someone had given our translator a rooster as an offering. People usually give bananas and such things but this time the translator managed to get a live rooster. Without us seeing, he put the rooster in a sack and got into the back seat of our car with the sack at his feet. As Mark and I climbed into the back seat, I asked Brother Mark if he would like to sit next to the window. He declined and sat in the middle. So the translator was on his left and I was sitting on his right. Mark was always the gentleman and under control, everything being done decently and in order.

All of a sudden I looked over at him and saw his body jerking from the waist down and his knees almost come up to his chest. In the darkness I thought Brother Mark was having some kind of physical problem. Then all of a sudden there was another jerk and he kept jerking and twisting. I said, "Mark is anything wrong?" He said, "No, brother." but I knew something was wrong. Then he asked me, in that very under control way he has, Brother, does you offer still hold to be able to sit by the window?"

I looked down and I realized a rooster was attacking his leg. It had gotten out of the sack. My mother didn't raise a fool. I looked at that rooster and I looked at his leg. I quickly replied, "No Mark, that offer only applied when we first got in the car."

Mark didn't know about the rooster until it had gotten out of the sack and started attacking him. As he was being scratched at he yelled for the translator to throw the rooster out of the window, but he refused. Chickens are valuable in India and the translator was somewhat rebellious. So the young man wrestled it back into the sack, but in the process the rooster hurt its head.

It ended up that the rooster was kept outside the window of the room at the hostel where we slept. For the next two days and nights the rooster crowed constantly because of its head injury. We couldn't get any sleep. Mark called it: "demon-possessed." The thing was just driving us crazy. Mark asked the translator to get rid of it, but he again refused.

Then one morning Mary Margaret, the Director of the hostel, called us to breakfast. Mark got to the breakfast table a few minutes before me and put two-and two together. There was chicken for breakfast. That was rare and most improbable in India. The rooster had stopped crowing that morning. Mark knew it was the "demon-possessed" rooster--fried and on the table. Mark wouldn't eat it but wanted to have a little fun with me. When I got to the table I sat down and was digging in when Mark said, "How do you like that fried chicken?" I said it was good but a little tough. Mark asked, "Did you notice that the rooster stopped crowing this morning?" A light bulb slowly came on over my head. I stopped chewing and a sick feeling swept over me. I was no longer hungry.

Mark said, "That'll teach you not to give me your seat!" We laughed and still laugh over it to this day.

Another thing that happened at the same hostel was when I decided to get some exercise. I went for a walk every afternoon the four days we were there. From the first day I went out, a nice little boy of about nine or ten started following me. He was very polite. On our walks together I saw some wild monkeys. There were about 30 of them. Coming from America it was amazing to see these monkeys. I asked the boy, "Do these monkeys come here every day? And he said, "Yes, Uncle." (Youth call you "Uncle" in India out of respect.)

I said, "They are beautiful monkeys, aren't they?"

"Yes, Uncle."

"Will they be back the same time tomorrow?"

"Yes, Uncle."

The next day some of his friends joined us on our walk, but the boy was always the spokesman. Everything I asked the boy he politely replied, "Yes, Uncle."

After our walk on the last day I just had to comment to the hostel administrator about how polite the boy was. She said, "Mr. Buza, you don't understand (she was trying to contain herself from laughing). The only English the boy knows is 'Yes' and 'Uncle.'" He didn't understand a word of what you were saying!"

When I returned to the United States I related this story in my home church in Syracuse. After I sat down Pastor Lee said, "Well Steve, I guess that young boy made a monkey's uncle out of you!"

10

The Salvation of Billy Shay

In the year 2000 Billy Shay turned 78 years old. He grew up and was a friend of my uncles. I knew Billy from the time I was eight years old. He was quite active in sports when I was a youngster along with my three uncles on the Evans side of the family. They were all very athletic in basketball and baseball.

Billy was a nice guy who never saw the need to give his life over to the Lord. A wonderful man and a tremendous gentleman but he never went to church or had any affiliations with a church. He never made time for the things of the Lord. He never married.

I found out through the family that he had been taken to the hospital four days earlier. I considered him an uncle, growing up around him like that, and

I held him in high regard. Once I found out he was in a brain dead coma at Community Hospital, the Holy Spirit rose up inside of me like other times that I was involved in brain dead cases. He spoke to my heart, "You've got to go to the hospital now and minister to him, only this is going to be different than what you have seen before. This time I am not going to raise him back from the dead."

I had a "word of knowledge" on the way there that I was going to lead him to the Lord before he died. I just knew I wasn't going to be used by the Lord to raise him back from the coma. God revealed to me that all his close family and friends would be there in the waiting room. I also knew they were un-churched people and it was going to be difficult to get in to see him. But on the way there the Holy Spirit also gave me a "word of wisdom." He said to my heart, "Before you ask them if you can go into Billy's room and minister to him, just sit and visit with them and have your Bible ready to turn to John 14: 1-14. I will give you an opportunity to share that passage of Scripture with them." I couldn't comprehend that they were going to let me share anything with them. I just went in obedience.

When I got to the hospital, things were exactly

as the Lord had shown me. I got very excited in my spirit that I had heard from the Lord so clearly. I walked in and there were the 10 or 12 people I knew would be there. They all knew me.

They said, "Steve what brings you here?" I told them I was concerned about Billy. I had heard what happened to him and I asked them to bring me up to date. I took about 15 minutes just showing my concern for the family and friends that were gathered there.

Billy had a brother named Jim. I sat in the only available chair next to Jim's wife. I started talking to the Lord in my heart: "Now Lord, you told me that I am going to get to share this passage of Scripture in John chapter 14 with them before I get a chance to see Billy." At that moment, out of a clear blue sky, Jim's wife says, "Steve, I see you have a Bible there." I said, "Yes, the Lord told me to bring my Bible with me and that I would need it to comfort you a little bit."

She said, "Can I ask you a question? We're not very religious people but as we were sitting here talking, just before you walked in, I went back to my Sunday school days. Like I said, I am not a religious person, but I was trying to tell the other folks here, isn't there a Scripture somewhere in the Bible where Jesus said he would go back to heaven and prepare a place for Billy?"

Amazed at how the Lord had been leading me, I responded: "I'm glad you asked because that happens to be the portion of Scripture that the Lord told me to get prepared to read to all of you. Can I take the time now to share it with you?"

She said, "Oh…by all means! I was trying to figure out what it was and I can't really remember it all."

I said, "Well you don't have to remember. Here it is in the Bible!"

With a tremendous excitement in my spirit, I quickly turned and read the full 14 verses to them.

She said, "That's the one! That's the one I was trying to tell you." She was very excited and proud that the Lord reminded her of something she learned in her childhood from the word of God.

With that the family opened up to me and saw that I had indeed been sent there by the Lord. It was now very easy. Jim's wife took me in to see Billy.

He had been brain dead for four days. The Lord told me on the way there that I would not be used to raise Billy from the dead. He just wanted to get Billy saved. So I stood there and I put my hand on his shoulder and said, "Billy, this is Steve Buza.

THE SALVATION OF BILLY SHAY

You know me very well. Obviously, I see that you are not doing too well. The doctors have been telling everybody that you are brain-dead. I just want you to know that I know that your spirit is very much alive and you can hear every word that I am saying to you. I am an ordained evangelist now since you have seen me last. I go all over the country and the world preaching the gospel of Jesus. I'm here as your friend and more importantly I am here as a minister of the gospel of Jesus Christ. The Lord spoke to me a few hours ago to come and minister to you because otherwise you are going to find yourself in hell for eternity. I am not trying to judge you, but even though you didn't let the Lord play a part in your life as you were living, He wants to play a very pivotal part in your life as you are dying. He is the same God that said to the thief on the cross in Luke 23:43: 'To day shalt thou be with me in paradise." The thief had done all kinds of things wrong, but he had enough sense to say, "Remember me when you come into your kingdom." Jesus told him that he would be with him in paradise that day. Jesus is saying that to you Billy. Today you can be with Jesus in paradise if you just listen to what I am talking about."

I continued, "I know that with your spirit you

can cry out. You can't use your vocal cords, but you have a spirit and you can reach out with your spirit to the Lord and you can pray in your spirit. I am now going to say a sinner's prayer of repentance and you just cry it out of your spirit to God."

I led him in a prayer something like this: "Dear Jesus, I confess to you that I am a sinner. I know that I have ignored you, Lord, my entire life, but I don't want to be lost and spend eternity in hell. I really don't deserve your forgiveness but Steve says you are a loving and forgiving God and that you do 'death-bed conversions.' Steve says you are willing to receive me into your kingdom. I am asking you right now, Jesus, to forgive all of my sins and wash me white as snow and make me your child, even at this late stage of my life. I receive you right now into my heart and I ask you to become my Lord and Savior. Amen."

After I prayed I noticed three more women from the waiting room had come in. Now there were two on one side of Billy's bed and two next to me. As we left the room I knew in my spirit that Billy was okay and that he was going to go to heaven.

A few days later my wife and I were at the funeral. As we walked into the wake for the viewing hours, a couple of the women who had been at the hospital came up to us. I had never seen people quite as excited as they were in my entire life.

"Steve, wasn't it wonderful? Did you see it? Did you see it? Did you see it?"

I thought that they were talking about how I had led him in the sinner's prayer. Don't they know that I saw it? After all, I was the one who prayed with him. But that wasn't what they were talking about.

I must have had a puzzled look on my face because they said, "You don't know what we are talking about, do you?"

"I guess I don't. You are going to have to help me out."

"From the first word out of your mouth we felt drawn to come in from the waiting room. We just couldn't stand the suspense any more. You probably didn't even realize we were there at the beginning because you had your eyes closed and your head bowed. But we were there from the first word out of your mouth. When you led him in the sinner's prayer all ten of his toes were moving frantically…wildly. Every single one of his toes. Not his body, just his toes. From the first word out of your mouth his toes were moving. We took it to be a sign from God that you were connecting with his spirit. The moment you said, "Amen," his toes went dead again and he was gone. You had to leave but we went back and told the rest of them in the waiting room. They agreed there was no way those toes could have been moving just when you were leading him in the sinners' prayer. He must have accepted the Lord even in a brain dead coma. That gave us such peace that shortly after you left we sent for the doctor. We told him we were ready to pull the plug because we know he's going home to be with Jesus Christ."

11

Moving Out in Ministry

Lessons from Pastor Lee

From 1997 to 2004, I had the honor of serving the Lord under Pastor Lee Simmons at Faith Chapel in Syracuse, New York. The Lord really gave me supernatural favor with Pastor Lee. And you need God's grace to get a mentor because they must see your potential and be willing to give you the time necessary to equip you for that next step in ministry.

I am so grateful for all the time that Pastor Lee spent with me. We played quite a bit of golf together. Many times we went to lunch together to talk about the things of the Lord. Sharon even noticed it and commented that the pastor and I had a great relationship. We had weekly afternoon appointments where we would pray and discuss issues together.

While I learned much traveling with Evangelist Mark Swiger during this same time period, we were only together a couple of months each year. The Lord put Pastor Lee with me to provide the training I needed in other areas.

While I had bold faith and was zealous for God I lacked wisdom and practical experience in applying my faith. Pastor Lee was used of the Lord mightily in my life to bring healing to my personality and smooth out my "rough edges."

When Sharon and I first came to Pastor Lee we had just left a bad situation in our former church. I felt I had to take a stand against some unrighteousness I saw exhibited in the leadership there. I'm the type of person that can't sweep things under the rug and just pretend everything is okay. We were hurt by the leaders and had to leave the church. We needed time to heal. Rather than just plug us into serving somewhere in his church right away, Pastor Lee just saw that we were just hurt and wounded sheep that needed time to heal. His compassion as a shepherd was very wonderful. We sat under a man who really cared about us as people and not just numbers to benefit his church.

MOVING OUT IN MINISTRY

It didn't matter how much of the gifting of the Lord I had in me, I still had to learn how to preach. Pastor Lee was a wonderful expositor of the Word of God to learn from. He knew I loved the Lord and had a lot of zeal but needed wisdom on how to "turn the corners." I could be very blunt and harsh in the way I presented things to people. He showed me how I could have softened the blows or done things a little more diplomatically. The Bible says, "Iron sharpens iron." Being mentored by Pastor Lee had this effect. It didn't rob me of my zeal, but it did hone away some of my rough edges.

One example that comes to mind was the first time he ever gave me a Wednesday night service. I was all excited to preach my first sermon there for him. I had done quite a bit of preaching before in other places but this was my first time at Faith Chapel so I really wanted to impress him.

Pastor Lee was sitting with his note pad paying close attention to my message. I'm thinking that he's taking notes because he is so impressed with my sermon. When I got all done, I walked over to him and asked, "How did you enjoy the sermon?" It was like sticking a needle into a fully inflated balloon. He said, "Well, if you sit down here, I'll dissect it with you. He said, "Your material was good. What you talked about was wonderful and I am sure the people were blessed, but do you see all these hash marks?"

I said, "I thought you were taking notes."

No, those marks are the 78 times in 35 minutes that you used the word "okay." God wants to heal you, okay. God's a loving God, okay. You didn't even know that you were saying that, did you?"

"I had no idea that I was using that expression so much."

"If you could get the 'okays' knocked out of your sermons you would be a tremendous preacher, but that is distracting people. I'm sorry I have to tell you but better I tell you now than you go the next twenty years with that flaw in your preaching."

Naturally, I was a little hurt. Sharon knew I was distraught on the way home after the service. It stung that my pastor had found such a glaring mistake. But I took it to the Lord in prayer for a little while. I told Pastor Lee, "Thank you for pointing it out to me and, with the help of the Holy Spirit, you will never hear me make that mistake again." From that time on he never heard the expression "okay" come out of my lips.

Pastor Lee helped my development in many ways. He allowed me to go with him to Jamaica on a mission trip where I was given opportunity to preach and heal the sick. I later served as an Elder at the church.

The Plentywood, Montana Campaign

Our friend and fellow evangelist Beth Nettles had invited us to come hold meetings in Plentywood, Montana. She knew a pastor there who phoned me and we set it up so that Beth and I would preach alternately for eleven days of meetings. As Sharon and I were on the flight there, I was very excited thinking: *Wow. God is finally opening up a major meeting where I can minister.* Just the honor of that was over-whelming. The Lord had been speaking to me that He was going to open up some doors, but when this one opened I was amazed at what a big door it was.

It was an icy and cold mid-October in 2002 when Beth met us at the airport in Minot, North Dakota. After we rented a car and had lunch at a Chinese restaurant we drove the three hours from

Minot to Sidney, Montana.

Our daughter Sherry lives with her husband and their two boys and two girls in Sidney. We stayed with them for a couple of days and then drove the 98 miles to Plentywood where the meetings were to be held.

Plentywood epitomizes the legend of the "Old West." Many outlaws hid out in the gulches surrounding the town. From there rustlers would drive their stolen cattle and horses on the "Outlaw Trail" across the border into Canada. At the site of present-day Plentywood, Sitting Bull and his Sioux people surrendered to the U. S. Army after living in Canada for five years. Plentywood today has a population of 1,700 people.

We arrived on Saturday at the lovely ranch home of Alice and Bob where we would be staying. He was a deacon in the church. They said we had the "freedom of the house" to have some rest time until the first service on Monday night.

The first two nights we held meetings at Pastor Greg's church. He was the host pastor and knew Beth well from her days when she was pastor of a church herself in Plentywood. Beth ministered the first night. The second night it was my turn.

I ministered on the healing power of Jesus

Christ. That was my topic. At the end of the service, I gave a demonstration of the gift of healing and the working of miracles. There were numerous spectacular healings. One in particular that stands out was a 13-year-old Indian girl.

After my message I gave an altar call for those who needed healing to come forward. So down the center aisle walked a mother and her little girl. She was the cutest little thing you ever saw. I could tell by the way she walked that she had a big problem. Her mother explained she had fallen off of a roof the year before. She and some other children were playing on a flat-roofed building on the reservation. As children do, they were clowning around when she accidentally stumbled off the 15-foot high building and went headfirst right to the ground. She was partially paralyzed. She now leaned at a 45-degree angle to her left from her waist up. She could walk, but very unnaturally. One leg had to drag to carry her body. They had taken her to about every surgeon in Montana. They said nothing could be done. If they tried to perform surgery on her she would be paralyzed and confined to a wheel chair for the rest of her life. She had a choice to be in a wheel chair or to live with the condition. It was slow-going and difficult for her to maneuver. It would have been a horrendous handicap to live with for the rest of her life.

So the mother had come to the meeting. She had heard about it through all the advertising. She came and sat with her daughter in the back until she saw some other miracles and the power of God. When she was convinced that this was really of God she brought her daughter down to the front for prayer. All I can tell you at this point in time is that supernatural faith came on me for this healing. I knew it wasn't going to be a recovery thing that would take six months or a year. It was like the Lord dropped a mantle of faith and authority on me so strong that the devil couldn't get near me. I just knew that this girl was going to receive a miracle and I told the mother so.

I said, "Can I have your permission as the mom to pray for your daughter?"

She said, "That's why I came to the service. You certainly can."

I said to the daughter, "Your mother has now given me permission to pray for you, but the Holy Spirit is a gentleman. Even though I have your mom's permission I want to know two things: One, do I have your permission to pray and two, do you believe that when I lay hands on your shoulder that

Jesus Christ will undo this tragic accident and give you a miracle?"

She said yes to the first question that I could pray for her, but on the second she just slumped her head like any 13 year-old kid would in that situation. I could just sense that she had lived with this for a year now and she didn't really have a whole lot of hope. To be honest with you, I think she thought this was too big, even for God.

I'll never forget what happened next. I said to her mom, "I am going to touch your daughter and, when I do, the power of the Holy Spirit of God is going to come on her and this entire church is going to see a miracle that they have never seen in their lifetime." I was prophesying to them that I knew this was coming. This wasn't "I think" this was going to happen. I told them, All of you get ready. You do not want to miss this!"

When I put my hands on the top of her shoulders all of a sudden her entire body just started to move back and move back and move back. Within 30 seconds, the Lord had straightened her back. She was standing totally straight, no longer leaning to the left.

I said to her, "Reach down and touch your toes."

She said that she couldn't.

I said, "That was then. This is now. Do what I tell you. Reach down and touch your toes."

She again said, "I can't."

I said, "You can. Do it now."

Her mother said, "Obey him. Do what he says."

She went down very, very carefully at first and she realized she could touch her toes. I told her she could do that faster. I had her do it six or seven times rapid fire, each time telling her "quicker, quicker." Eventually she had her palms right on the floor. The people there went absolutely out of their minds with joy.

The word of that miracle soon spread throughout town because everybody knew about her accident. In a community that size everybody knows everyone else. Because of the crowds we overflowed the church and had to move the last nine meetings to the largest venue in town, the civic center.

In the meetings, Beth and I let the Holy Spirit lead us. Beth did her sermons and I did mine, but no matter which one of us ministered, we always asked each other to come up on the platform at the end. There were so many responding for prayer that we needed to minister together.

There were many wonderful miracles that happened, but the one I share next stands out as something from which we all can learn.

We were into the ninth meeting. I was about 10 or 15 minutes into my sermon when I spotted a lady that was sitting in the center aisle. This was highly unusual because usually I don't stop a sermon to minister to somebody. The Holy Spirit just had me stop and I said, "Young lady. Yes, you in the red dress. Come up here right now. I have a word for you." This was a step of faith for me because all that the Lord told me was, "You have a word for her."

Now it took a while for her to walk from where she was up to where I was. I had nothing to give her but I was obedient to the prompting of the Holy Spirit.

As she was walking toward me, I was nervously talking to the Holy Spirit saying, "It sure would be a good idea if you would tell me what I am supposed to tell this woman before I make a fool out of myself here." This was a learning process for me. I learned that when the Holy Spirit tells you that you've got a word it doesn't necessarily mean He is going to give it to you in advance.

She came up and then the Holy Spirit started speaking to me. "Have her turn and face the congregation." I asked her to please turn and face the people and then He says, "Tell her this is not meant to embarrass her, but I have a purpose for this and tell her everything is going to be okay and to relax and not be embarrassed." I gave her those directions.

Then I sort of turned sideways and I told her, "Here's the word of the Lord for you, young lady," and as I am saying that I am thinking it better keep coming because I had no idea of what was coming next. Then all of a sudden, it just came like water from a fire hose. It was just pumping right out of me. I was just on autopilot now. It was all God and no Steve whatsoever. I said, "Here's the word of the Lord to you. This is not to bring condemnation. God has great glory He is going to get out of what we are doing right here now or He wouldn't have interrupted this sermon. You made a pledge a while back to a well-known evangelist, and unlike a pledge that is normally for 12 months, this one was only a 10-month pledge. I don't know the evangelist and I don't know the amount because the Lord is not showing me but here's what I do know: You sat down the next day and wrote out less than half of what that first monthly pledge check was supposed to be and you wanted to immediately rip up the check and just throw it away. You thought that your pledge was just an emotional reaction when you saw him on TV. Am I correct so far?" She said, "You are very correct so far."

Her eyes got big like saucers. She was astonished. I said, "You did send the check. You didn't rip it up. Is that right?" She said, "That's right. You haven't missed anything yet." I told her, "Here is what the Lord wants you to do. Tomorrow morning do the math and figure out how much that first check was short, make up the difference, put it in the mailbox immediately tomorrow morning. Beth and I are here only three more days, and if you obey this word, you will see the glory of God. In other words, before we leave town you will see the intervention of God with a bona fide miracle for you." I said, "Will you do that?" She said, "I will do that." I told her thank you and she went back to her seat and I continued on with my sermon.

The next night when we came back, it was Beth's night to minister, but before she started I went up and took the microphone.

"Young lady, the one that was up here last night. Please come up here right now. Take this microphone and tell the people what happened in your life today."

She said, "For those of you who were not here last night, Evangelist Steve told me that I had written out less than half of the first payment I had pledged to a TV evangelist. He said he didn't know the amount or the evangelist but I am going to tell you tonight. It was Benny Hinn. Steve was correct that it wasn't a one-year pledge. It was a ten-month pledge just like he said. That was an unusual amount of time. Normally pledges are one year's time. It was for $58 a month and I sent in $ 23 instead of $58. So it was less than half of what it was supposed to be. I did send it in just like he said. I was blown away last night knowing that there was no way he could have known that stuff without a word of knowledge from the Holy Spirit. He never met me before and there was no way in a thousand lifetimes he could have known that information had the Lord not given it to him. I am not the smartest person in the world, but I knew I better obey the man of God. This morning I got up bright and early, did the math, figured out what it was and wrote the check out. This time I joyfully put the check in the mailbox and put the red flag up."

She continued, "Somewhere around 11:30, a man that I rarely run into and don't know very well came up the sidewalk and rang the doorbell and said he had something for me. He handed me an envelope and just left. He definitely was not in the meeting last night. I went into the house and I was a little bit shaken that this may be a 'God-connection.' I poured myself a cup of coffee, opened up the envelope and in it was a check made out from him to me for $580. It was just exactly to the penny what my entire ten-month pledge was. I remember Brother Steve saying, 'Before we leave town, if you obey you will see the glory of God.' It gets better than this. This afternoon, another woman came up and said that the Lord had told her to give something to me and she handed me $300 in cash. Now I have money above and beyond what it took to meet the pledge. I am just lit right up. I'm glowing like a light bulb!"

I was to minister on the last night of the campaign. While I was preparing my message for that night, the Holy Spirit spoke to my heart very clearly and said, "Son, tonight I am going to take you to a new level."

I said, "Lord, tell me what you are going to do."

"All I am going to give you now is the sermon for tonight. I will tell you what to do later. I am not going to show you right now."

Looking back I know why he didn't show me. I would have been so anxious had I known in advance that I would have been pacing like a caged lion.

That night I basically preached a normal sermon. On every other night Beth and I had ministered together at the end of each service. When people came forward for prayer we prayed for anything and everything. Not just physical healing, anything. But this night the Holy Spirit just checked me and said, "Tell Beth to stay right there. Don't call her up. Tell the people to stay in their seats. Tell them not to come up and that you are going to do something different tonight." The Lord spoke to me that afternoon that there was going to be a very unusual ending to this service. So I am getting this as I am going along. The Lord is just showing me a piece at a time.

The civic center was a metal, insulated building with a flat-style roof. Standing on the platform and facing the crowd there was a big wing that went at an angle to my left and a big wing that went at an angle to my right. There was a large center section in the middle.

He said, "Talk to the people on the left hand section and tell all of the sick to stand to their feet. Tell everybody near them, around them or behind them to get right up tight to them. Point at them one at a time starting from the front and going to the last one in the back. As you point to them, I am going to touch them and heal them. Tell the people behind them to hold on to them because if not there are going to be chairs that are flying and people will get hurt."

So I gave them that directive and just started pointing. Boom…boom…boom…They were just being slain in the Spirit the second my finger even got close to where they were. People were having all they could do to keep the sick from crashing in a heap on the floor.

Then the Lord directed me, "Move to the center section. Point quicker to the ones in the center section. I am going to do it quicker now."

So I really started pointing quickly to them. Boom…boom…boom…boom…in a matter of no time they all fell out in the power of God.

The Lord then led me to move to the right-hand section and spoke to me: "I want to show the people my glory before you leave town. Have them stand up just like the other two sections, but the minute the last one is up just wave at them. I am going to touch them all at one time."

I had them all stand and told them to concentrate on the Lord and not on me. I just waved and the whole section went down like wheat blowing in the wind. It was over that quick.

People were healed, blessed and amazed at the power of God. What a wonderful way to end the campaign!

Epilogue

After 40 years of "on-the-job" training, God has released me to serve Him as an evangelist full-time. My son has taken over the Buza family business.

I found the number 40 has great significance in the Bible. Moses was in training on the backside of the desert for 40 years before God sent him to Egypt to free His people. Our Lord Jesus was 40 days in the wilderness right before he started his ministry in power. The children of Israel wandered for 40 years until a generation arose that believed God for His promises.

I believe I also have been in training for "such a time as this." The nations are ripe for the great End Time Harvest. As the children of Israel cried out to God for deliverance from the bonds of Egypt, people today are crying out for freedom from the chains of Satan—freedom from demonic oppression, sickness, mental torments, and poverty of soul and spirit. The world is ripe for revival.

My wife Sharon and I stand ready to serve your church, community, or nation in seeing people set free to know the Lord. Please feel free to contact me to minister at your church, evangelistic campaign, healing seminar or conference.

Rev. Steve Buza
www.stevebuza-ministries.org